50
management
ideas
you really need to know

Edward Russell-Walling

Quercus

Contents

Introduction *3*

01 Adhocracy *4*
02 Balanced scorecard *8*
03 Benchmarking *12*
04 Blue ocean strategy *16*
05 Boston matrix *20*
06 BPR *24*
07 Brand *28*
08 Channel management *32*
09 Core competence *36*
10 Corporate governance *40*
11 Corporate social responsibility *44*
12 Corporate strategy *48*
13 Costs of complexity *52*
14 Customer relationship management *56*
15 Decentralization *60*
16 Diversification *64*
17 The 80:20 principle *68*
18 Empowerment *72*
19 Entrepreneurship *76*
20 Experience curve *80*
21 The five forces of competition *84*
22 The four Ps of marketing *88*
23 Globalization *92*
24 Innovation *96*
25 Japanese management *100*

26 The knowledge economy *104*
27 Leadership *108*
28 Lean manufacturing *112*
29 The learning organization *116*
30 The long tail *120*
31 Loyalty *124*
32 Management by objectives *128*
33 Market segmentation *132*
34 Mergers and acquisitions *136*
35 Organizational excellence *140*
36 Outsourcing *144*
37 Project management *148*
38 Scientific management *152*
39 Six Sigma *156*
40 Stakeholders *160*
41 Strategic alliances *164*
42 Supply chain management *168*
43 Systems thinking *172*
44 Theories X & Y (and Theory Z) *176*
45 Tipping point *180*
46 Total quality management *184*
47 Value chain *188*
48 War and strategy *192*
49 Web 2.0 *196*
50 What business are you really in? *200*

Glossary *204*
Index *206*

Introduction

Companies are much like people, if you don't look too closely. You get a few kind thoughtful ones, a few grasping ugly ones, and many shades in between. Like the rest of us, they want to get on, earn more and influence others. And they think about how to do all that – a lot. A handful of them have enough confidence and self-knowledge to work it out for themselves. Others feel happier going to a professional for advice. The rest, and there are plenty of them, wait to see what everyone else is doing and then copy their ideas.

Original or borrowed, those ideas are the subject of this book. They may be about overall strategy – how the company plans to get to where it wants to be. Some are about styles of management. Others look at organization – how the company structures itself and arranges its systems. There are different management ideas on how to compete, motivate people or improve quality, on leadership and even on ways of thinking.

Management ideas are a product, like any other. They often begin as practice inside innovative companies, but they are usually hammered into theories – manufactured as ideas – inside the business schools. From there they go to idea retailers, the management and business consultants, who distribute them among the corporate population at large. Companies put the ideas to work and give feedback on any faults, the academics tweak the design and, if it's a sound idea, the cycle continues.

Like any other product, ideas have a value, which can be high, especially when they are shiny and new. But they also have a shelf life. An eye-catching idea becomes the hottest management must-have for a while and then sinks from view, as managers realize it didn't really do what it said on the tin. Some are better than others and become part of the mainstream, adapted for new times. Other hot properties are overhyped and oversold, then fall from grace, though some of their essence survives as part of accepted thought. This continual cycle of new lamps for old is perpetuated partly by the academics and consultants, who need new product flow if they are to have a business at all, and partly by demand from managements, with their robust appetite for anything that promises to make their businesses better.

Management has never quite decided whether it's an art or a science. Science promises certainty, which is an elusive quality in modern business, and managers would dearly love to have a little more of it. It's that lack of product guarantee, in a world that insists on changing, that will keep new management ideas bubbling up, continually adding to the evolutionary diversity that I hope this book reveals.

01 Adhocracy

As organizational structures go, adhocracy is the direct opposite of bureaucracy – unstructured, decentralized and, at least in theory, responsive. In a bureaucracy, the structure is more important than the people. An adhocracy, on the other hand, is designed to bring out the best in them.

A bureaucracy is 'a hierarchical administrative system designed to deal with large quantities of work in a routine manner, largely by adhering to a set of strict and impersonal rules', according to the *Oxford Dictionary of Business and Management*. 'It is characterized by its permanence and stability, its body of experience and precedent, and its absence of a reliance on individuals.' Which more or less sums up what an adhocracy is not.

The idea first surfaced in the work of US leadership theorist Warren G. Bennis. Writing about the company of the future in *The Temporary Society* (with Philip Slater in 1968), he predicted that it would rely on nimble and flexible project teams within a structure he called 'adhocracy'. The Latin phrase ad hoc means 'for this particular purpose only', though today it also conveys a sense of improvization.

> **'Adhocracy is organised chaos.'**
>
> **Alvin Toffler, 1970**

The idea of adhocracies received a more dramatic boost from Alvin Toffler in his 1970 bestseller *Future Shock*. In it, he saw them as 'a new, free-form world of kinetic organizations', predicting that firms would need flatter structures, faster information flows and disposable project teams in order to survive. Next it was Henry Mintzberg's turn to seize on the term. Mintzberg, who made his name studying how managers really spend their

timeline

1450
Innovation

1920
Decentralization

Mintzberg's organizations (and coordination mechanisms)

	Simple	Complex
Stable	**Machine Bureaucracy** Standardized work processes and outputs	**Professional Bureaucracy** Standardized skills and norms
Dynamic	**Entrepreneurial Startup** Direct supervision	**Adhocracy** Mutual adjustment

time, also thought about organizational structures. In his 1979 book *The Structuring of Organizations* (among others), he identified four fundamental types. These were determined using a two-by-two matrix that plotted the nature of their work environment (simple or complex) against their pace of change (stable or dynamic). The resulting classifications were the machine bureaucracy, the professional bureaucracy, the entrepreneurial startup and the adhocracy. Mintzberg argues that each uses fundamentally different mechanisms to coordinate its activities, adding that power resides among different groups within each type.

The machine bureaucracy This has highly specialized but routine operating tasks, formal procedures, lots of self-generated rules and regulations, formalized communication, large operating units and relatively centralized decision-making. It also has a lot of what Mintzberg calls 'technostructure' – platoons of managers, planners and accountants. The coordination mechanism is the standardization of procedures and outputs – and that is the responsibility of the technocrats. So they wield considerable power. Think General Motors.

The most influential people in a professional bureaucracy are the highly trained professionals at its operating core. They work relatively

In clover

Management theory and innovation has always been dominated by Americans, because the US has the largest concentration of business in the world, and therefore the largest market for it. But the UK has made the occasional sparkling contribution, not least from Charles Handy, a former Shell executive and London Business School professor. One of Handy's many thought-provoking ideas has been the 'shamrock organization'.

Expounded in *The Age of Unreason* (1989), the shamrock is a post-adhocratic structure that reflects the growing flexibility and fragmentation of many modern organizations. The people within one of Handy's shamrock organizations are grouped into three separate leaves.

First, there is the **core workforce** of full-time professional managers and administrators, well-paid, hard-working, small in number.

Then there is the **contractual fringe**. These are skilled contractors, hired as and when the company needs them, without paying their overheads. They are paid a fee to produce a specified result, though their methods may be beyond the company's control.

Finally, there is the **flexible labour** force of part-timers and temporary staff. The company prefers to have these lower-paid workers carrying out supporting tasks rather than its expensive core workers.

independently. Like the machine bureaucracy, they are rule-bound, but whereas the former sets its own rules, the professionals' standards – the coordination mechanism – come from an outside body. Think hospitals or a large accounting firm.

The entrepreneurial startup This is low on technostructure but high in centralized power, invariably in the hands of the founder or chief executive. So the coordination mechanism takes the form of direct supervision and control, and the boss and senior managers wield most influence. This type of organization tends to be flexible and informal, inspiring loyalty while not doing much in the way of planning. Most firms pass through this stage in their early years.

> **❛As the monolithic "palace" structures of corporations give way, we are being thrust into a world of tents.❜**
> **Charles Handy, 1999**

> **❝The adhocracy shows the least reverence for the classical principles of management.❞**
> **Henry Mintzberg, 1979**

The adhocracy has nothing in common with the machine bureaucracy. Instead, it shares the informality of the startup with the devolved responsibility of the professional bureaucracy, though often to a greater extent than either. As Bennis suggested, their specialists have considerable autonomy and are deployed in small, market-based project teams. Since innovation and creativity are central to the business, the level of standardization and rule-making is low. Coordination depends on the mutual adjustment of ad hoc teams, so no particular unit is disproportionately powerful. Much of the latter-day IT industry is organized on adhocratic lines, as are advertising agencies and new media companies.

Mintzberg distinguished between two kinds of adhocracy. The operating adhocracy innovates and solves problems for its clients – like the aforementioned software houses and ad agencies. The administrative adhocracy has the same project team structure but operates to serve itself – Mintzberg offers the National Aeronautics and Space Administration (NASA) as an example. In an administrative adhocracy, low-level operations may be automated or contracted out.

Adhocracy is alive and well. Robert Waterman, co-author of *In Search of Excellence*, published another book simply called *Adhocracy* in 1990. He defined adhocracy as 'any form of organization that cuts across normal bureaucratic lines to capture opportunities, solve problems and get results'. And he argued that, in an age of accelerating change, organizations such as these, with their ability to adapt and adjust, were the most likely to succeed.

the condensed idea
The opposite of bureaucracy

02 Balanced scorecard

If management were a sports team, strategy would be the hero calling the plays who gets all the column inches. But strategy means nothing if it's not carried out successfully. So performance measurement and management, humble team players, are just as important in getting points on the board. Since the early 1990s, a favoured tool for keeping a grip on implementation has been the balanced scorecard.

The balanced scorecard (BSC) has been through various stages of evolution since then, but it was first articulated in a 1992 *Harvard Business Review* article by Robert S. Kaplan and David Norton. BSC takes an organization's strategy, separates it into quantifiable goals and then measures whether the goals are being achieved. It starts with vision – mission statement, perhaps – and breaks that down into strategies, then tactical activities and concludes with metrics. It's the structure of the metrics – the measuring activities – that is 'balanced'.

Kaplan later wrote a book called *The Balanced Scorecard: You Can't Drive a Car Solely Relying on a Rearview Mirror*, which says it all in a nutshell. The two academics didn't deny the need for financial statistics as an aid to navigation and to keep the shareholders calm, but insisted that other perspectives were necessary. They added another three, giving them four in total.

timeline

1965	1985
Corporate strategy	Value chain

> **The Balanced scorecard describes the theory of your strategy. You believe that, if you do A, B will happen. So you now have to start monitoring the strategy through your feedback systems . . . testing the hypothesis. You should always ask the question, if I am doing A, is B happening?**

David Norton, 2001

The financial perspective 'How do we look to shareholders?' Few companies suffer from a shortage of financial information. The organization's financial performance is fundamental to its survival and to satisfying its shareholders. So accurate data such as return on capital employed, unit costs, cash flow, market share and profit growth remain very important bearings on the company's progress. Kaplan and Norton had little criticism of this aspect of measurement other than to suggest that there was sometimes too much of it. They emphasized, however, that financial data is, by definition, historical. It tells us what has happened to the organization. It may not be as effective as telling us what is happening to the organization right now. And, as they say in financial advertising, past performance is no guarantee of future success.

The customer perspective 'How do we look to customers?' Kaplan and Norton were writing at a time when companies were growing more aware of a need to see things from the customer's point of view, and acknowledging the truth that it costs a lot more to find a new customer than to keep an existing one. 'Customer satisfaction' was developing into a mantra and 'customer relationship management' was about to become the next fashionable management idea – and concern for the customer has certainly not decreased since then. To view the business from this perspective, the company must gauge how satisfied customers are with the

Kaplan and Norton

The balanced scorecard is one of the most popular management ideas of recent times. One consulting firm recently estimated that at least 40% of the Fortune 1000 companies were using the methodology.

Its authors, Robert S. Kaplan and David Norton, have published a number of books and established a prosperous consultancy business that helps companies to implement their ideas. Kaplan is a professor at Harvard Business School, where he has taught since 1984, and was featured in the *Financial*

Times list of Top 25 Business Thinkers in 2005. Norton is the professional consultant of the partnership and runs BSCol, the company they founded together.

In *The Strategy-Focused Organization*, which appeared in 2001, they upgraded the balanced scorecard into a 'strategic management system', introducing their so-called 'strategy map'. A one-page diagram incorporating the four BSC perspectives, Kaplan says the map is 'a model of how an organization creates value'.

products and service they receive. Measurement here includes customer satisfaction, customer retention rates, response rates and reputation.

The business process perspective 'How effective are we internally?' This is an inward-looking, internal perspective, measuring the performance of all those key processes that drive the business. For many companies, particularly those in manufacturing, this was more familiar ground, the realm of people holding stopwatches and clipboards. The measures themselves would depend on the nature of the business but might include manufacturing excellence and quality, time to get new products to market and inventory management. Some frame the question that this perspective seeks to answer: 'What must we excel at?'

> **'Once you describe it, you can manage it.'**
> **David Norton, 2001**

The learning and growth perspective 'How can we change and improve?' Answers to this question give a measure of potential future performance, focusing on the need to invest in the development of the organization's people. 'Learning' encompasses more than merely 'training', though it includes that too. Hours spent on training and the number of employee suggestions might be among the measures sought. But Kaplan and Norton also promote the idea of mentors and tutors within the firm, as well as a relaxed style of communication between employees that allows them to get help with problems when needed. Some include innovation in this perspective, adding measures such as research and development as a proportion of sales, for example, or the percentage of sales from new products.

Put the data from these four different points of view together and the results do what it says on the packet – they give a 'balanced' view of the organization, rather than an overwhelmingly financial one. The link between measurement and strategy comes in the choice of what gets measured – the metrics. But BSC doesn't stop at measurement. The point of measurement is to allow managers to see the organization more clearly, and to manage more effectively – to take better decisions – based on that information.

So Kaplan and Norton, who have built a profitable business out of helping companies to implement BSC, maintain that it is a management as well as a measurement system. They say you can't improve what you can't measure. Feedback from the scorecard is used to adapt the implementation of strategy or, if necessary, strategy itself.

Today, BSC is still widely used among large companies and has gained a following among public sector and non-profit organizations. Some users note that, carried out properly, BSC can be a catalyst for change. They point out that the performance measurement is not an end in itself. As Goodhart's law suggests, measures should not become targets. Instead, they should serve as aids to analysis. They don't have to be accurate, but people must have confidence in them as reliable indicators of what is actually going on.

> **'Financial systems are always snapshots: they can't describe a time-based logic of cause and effect. They can't integrate different kinds of assets into what I would call a strategic recipe.'**
>
> **David Norton,** 2001

the condensed idea
An all-round view of the business

03 Benchmarking

If someone is doing something more successfully than you are, it makes sense to look over their shoulder and see what you can learn from them. US manufacturers started doing this when they realized that Japanese competitors were taking away their markets. It's called benchmarking and it's become so widespread among big companies that some business thinkers now caution against it.

The history books point to Xerox as being the first large US corporation to benchmark. That was in the late 1970s when, like many of its compatriots, it was feeling the competitive heat. It took all the key parts of the business, from production to sales and maintenance, and measured them against their counterparts in other companies, abroad as well as at home. If the performance of the other's process was better in some way – quicker, cheaper, more efficient – Xerox determined at least to match it. In so doing, it transformed its own overall performance and word spread. So did the practice of benchmarking.

Another famous early benchmarking exercise was the International Motor Vehicle Programme, which ran from 1985–90. Coordinated at the Massachusetts Institute of Technology and involving US, European and Japanese automobile manufacturers, it sought to establish why the Japanese were performing so much better than everyone else. The conclusions led to the adoption in the west of what is now known as lean manufacturing (see page 112).

A benchmark is a standard of performance; it can apply to anything from production rates and defect levels to how you answer the phone. In benchmarking, you first assess your own performance, compare it with

timeline

1940s	1951
Lean marketing	Total quality management

others and, if they are superior, you do what it takes to match or – better – exceed it. The Japanese, interestingly enough, don't have a word for it but, in the spirit of continuous improvement, they do it constantly. There was a time when no western trade show was complete without squads of earnestly polite young Japanese scribbling in notebooks.

Inside and out Benchmarking comes in different forms. Internal benchmarking may compare the way service departments in different regions handle warranty claims, for example. If nothing else, that can be a good way to find out how benchmarking works. External benchmarking is harder and should be more productive. Doing it with direct competitors can be delicate, since they will be reluctant to share certain information, though in certain areas – like health and safety – competitors may be more cooperative for the sake of the industry as a whole.

Beyond your market Benchmarking against practices in unrelated industries is easier and usually more useful, since it is more likely to tell you things you didn't know. Looking beyond one's own industry helps to remove blinkers and – when it comes to implementation – is less likely to fall foul of the 'not invented here' syndrome. British airport operator BAA provided a classic example of cross-industry benchmarking when it compared notes with Ascot racecourse and Wembley football stadium. It reasoned, with great good sense, that they too had to cope with mass arrivals and departures over short periods of time.

Step by step Benchmarking methodologies vary in detail but follow much the same route. **Pick a benchmark**. It shouldn't be too broad in scope, and should be capable of precise definition. One school of thought says that everything can and should be benchmarked but this becoming a minority view, given the cost in time and people. For that same reason, commitment from the top is important. Then **pick a team**. Some companies favour small teams of two or three, others more, but at least

> **The most significant cost [of benchmarking] will be the management time.**
> Oxford Dictionary of Business and Management, 2006

1970s — Benchmarking | 1985 — Value chain | 2004 — Blue ocean strategy

Black marks

Benchmarking has been taken up in Australia as enthusiastically as anywhere else. Aussie benchmarkers particularly like the story of the concrete supplier who benchmarked against a pizza parlour, in an effort to improve its delivery times. Benchmarking Plus, a Melbourne-based consultancy, offers this advice on what not to do:

Don't confuse benchmarking with taking part in a survey – surveying companies in your industry may tell you where you rank, but won't improve your position. Surveys may give interesting numbers, but benchmarking tells us what is behind the numbers.

Don't confuse benchmarking with research – benchmarking is for existing processes. If you are starting a new process and looking at other company's ideas, that's research.

Don't take on too much – if a process is a group of tasks and a system is a group of processes, don't try to benchmark a total system. It will take too long, cost too much and it will be hard to stay focused.

Don't underestimate the importance of having the right partner – research benchmarking partners thoroughly. Don't waste their time or yours.

Don't neglect your homework – know your own process thoroughly and know what you want to learn before approaching partners.

Don't misalign – don't choose a topic that is not aligned with the overall business goals or that cuts across some existing initiative.

some should be senior enough to get their recommendations approved. Outside consultants can be used, particularly if confidentiality is an issue or the company is inexperienced. Either way, the first step is to **analyse your own process** from beginning to end, so that you know what is being benchmarked. For those who think they know their own processes, this can yield surprising results and may prove a benefit in itself.

Select partners – this is not always straightforward, as the most obvious or attractive may well be suffering from benchmark fatigue. **Decide on measurement methods** and – important – units, and then **collect the data**. The data report should include any differences in the partner's practices and structure as well as its processes. **Analyse the results** and, in the jargon, **determine the 'gap'**.

Then **plan for change**, identifying any ideas you can adopt or adapt to improve your own process and determining how to implement them. The plans should aim to take you well beyond the present gap. The next time you compare notes – which you should – the partner will presumably have continued to improve as well.

Why you shouldn't This benchmarking model has become so embedded as standard practice that, unsurprisingly, some voices are now being raised against it. One argument is that such effort represents poor use of management time, which could be better spent thinking about the fundamentals in one's own company.

> **❛ Copying best practices may make you more efficient, but it will also make you look more like your competitors. ❜**
> **Nicolaj Siggelkow,** 2006

Daniel Levinthal of the Wharton business school's management department acknowledges that benchmarking can have value and power, but warns that there may be dangers in imitating some policies and practices of other firms. He points out that the different functional components of a firm are both complementary and reinforcing – 'interdependent'. Firms that have sustained their competitive advantage over time are the ones that are good at managing those interdependencies.

The implicit assumption of benchmark thinking is that the policy adopted from outside can be independent of everything else the firm is doing. However, for one these components – human resources, say – to adopt the best management practice of another company may not only not be best for the firm, but may actually be dysfunctional. It could disturb the internal consistency of the company's interlocking set of strategy choices.

Finally, there is mounting criticism of the way in which benchmarking is making all companies look the same, producing strategic convergence. And lack of differentiation, as Michael Porter would say, is no source of competitive advantage.

the condensed idea
Keeping up

04 Blue ocean strategy

Innovate! Innovate! Hardly a new idea. Everyone knows that the dream business strategy is to create a new product that everyone wants and no one else is offering, but that's easier said than done. How do you do it? W. Chan Kim and Renée Mauborgne think they have an answer, a framework to help companies swim free of the threshing, bloody red ocean of competition into calm and uninfested waters – the blue ocean.

Ever since Michael Porter, most companies have built their strategies around the idea of competition. But Porter's theories of competitive advantage through differentiation or cost leadership have been so persuasive that they have become a given. Everybody does it. Strategic and operational benchmarking has given us not differentiation but a bland international conformity. Oversupply of commoditized products, static if not falling demand and declining brand loyalties have led to price wars and shrinking profit margins. This is the known market space, limited and fought over, the red ocean. The blue ocean is the unknown, uncontested market space. Others have created blue oceans for themselves, and Kim and Mauborgne insist that companies stuck in the red ocean can do the same. These two are professors of strategy and international management at the INSEAD business school. They sketched out their ideas in a paper entitled 'Blue ocean strategy' in 2004 and followed it up with a book the following year, describing how to implement them.

> **'When a company's strategy is formed reactively as it tries to keep up with the competition, it loses its uniqueness.'**
> **W. Chan Kim and Renée Mauborgne, 2005**

timeline

1450	1924
Innovation	Market segmentation

Circus performers The most striking example of a business that has colonized the blue ocean is the captivating Cirque du Soleil, the Canadian travelling circus for grown-ups. The circus was a dying trade when Cirque du Soleil was created in 1984. Children had better things to do on their games consoles and animal rights groups had circuses in their sights. So Cirque du Soleil stopped trying to beat the competition. Instead of trying to procure more famous (and more expensive) clowns, it created a new market for a new group of customers – who were happy to pay a lot more. Nearly 40 million people have since been to 'The Circus'.

Other denizens of their own blue oceans include Pret a Manger, which serves quality eats at fast-food speed; Curves, an affordable, women-only health club chain; and JC Decaux, which energized outdoor advertising in the 1960s by creating street furniture. Kim and Mauborgne claim strategic logic singles out these and other blue ocean companies, calling it 'value innovation'.

Value creation on its own is usually incremental, and innovation alone tends to be technology-driven and too futuristic for consumers to accept readily. Value innovation makes competition irrelevant by creating a leap in value for buyers and the company. It anchors innovation with value, aligning it with utility, price and cost. It doesn't make the Porter-esque choice between differentiation and low cost, but pursues them simultaneously.

> **To focus on the red ocean is . . . to accept the key constraining factors of war – limited terrain and the need to beat an enemy to succeed.**
> **W. Chan Kim and Renée Mauborgne,** 2005

The sailing manual Blue ocean strategy formulation follows four principles.

1. Reconstruct market boundaries Look for blue oceans where the competition isn't looking – in industries that provide alternatives to your products; among users as opposed to purchasers or influencers; in complementary services (like post-sales maintenance); in emotional or functional appeal; or across time, by anticipating trends.

Causing distribution

Innovation, much prized by management thinkers, can put others out of business. Technology that eventually destroys the dominant product is known as 'disruptive' and its chief chronicler is Harvard professor Clayton Christensen.

Disruptive innovation, as Christensen points out in *The Innovator's Dilemma*, takes a number of forms. One is 'low-end' disruption, where the existing product exceeds the requirements of certain customers. The new product enters the market at this less profitable end, with a quality that is just good enough. Early digital cameras, for example, had low picture quality but were cheap. With its foothold, the disruptor then needs to improve its profit margin and so increases quality. The incumbent doesn't work too hard to defend share in this still none-too-profitable segment, and withdraws upmarket to concentrate on its higher-value customers

Christensen says that it is gradually squeezed in this way until the disruptor's quality satisfies the most profitable end of the market. Lights out.

'New market' disruptors have an inferior performance by most standards but fit an emerging segment. The Linux operating system fitted this description. Other disruptors are superior but ignored by existing players, who defend their investments in the older technology. By refusing to modernize when the more efficient containerization method came along, the port of San Francisco lost out to the port of Oakland.

One of the litmus tests of disruptive technologies is that they invariably enable a larger population of less skilled people to do things that historically only an expert could do. But, says Christensen, you can't disrupt a market where customers are not yet over-served by the prevailing offerings.

NetJets, the creator of fractional jet ownership, looked across alternative markets and broke the tradeoff between owning an executive jet and flying first class. Home Depot did the same by providing professional home decorator advice at prices that were lower than the hardware store's. In Japan, where men's haircuts were emotionally driven, time-consuming and expensive, QB House made them functional, quick and cheap. Swatch changed the functionally driven budget watch into an emotionally driven fashion statement.

2. Focus on the big picture, not the numbers Kim and Mauborgne describe how to draw up a 'strategy canvas' instead of drowning in spreadsheets and budgets.

3. Reach beyond existing demand Instead of concentrating on customers, look at non-customers. Callaway Golf discovered that many people didn't play golf because hitting the ball was too hard. So it designed a golf club with a bigger head.

4. Get the strategic sequence right Build the strategy in the following order. If the answer to any of these is no, you need to rethink:

• Buyer utility – is there exceptional buyer utility in your business idea? Utility is not the same as amazing technology.
• Price – is your price easily accessible to the mass of buyers? Traditional innovation launches start high and come down (it's called 'skimming'). But in the blue ocean it is important to know from the start what price will quickly attract the mass of target buyers. Volume generates higher returns than it used to and, for buyers, the value of a product may be closely tied to the number of people using it.
• Cost – can you hit your cost target and make a profit at your strategic price?
• Adoption – What are the hurdles to adoption and are you addressing them up front? Blue ocean ideas threaten the status quo and may inspire fear and resistance among employees, business partners and the public. Educate the fearful.

Kim and Mauborgne round off their theory with advice on how to implement it. Whether or not it stays the course as a methodology, it is an enlightening contribution to post-Porter literature.

> **Value innovation is a new way of thinking about and executing strategy that results in the creation of a blue ocean and a break from the competition.**
> W. Chan Kim and Renée Mauborgne, 2005

the condensed idea
Making competition irrelevant

05 Boston matrix

The Boston matrix is the Marlon Brando of management tools – brilliant, fêted, poorly deployed and then discredited, but still illuminating in the right context. Otherwise known as the 'growth/share matrix' it is, according to one management writer, one of the 'two most powerful tools in the history of strategy'.

Companies can use the Boston Matrix to analyse their portfolio of businesses and then to decide what to do with them – spend money on building them up, simply keep them ticking over or dump them. Sometimes referred to as the BCG matrix, it was developed in the late 1960s by Bruce Henderson of the Boston Consulting Group – hence its name. Henderson and his colleagues were also responsible for the other of those 'two most powerful tools' – the experience curve (see page 80).

In mathematics, a matrix is a table of numbers used to compute a solution. More traditionally, it's a mould, used to cast vinyl records for the music industry or printing type. In the case of the Boston matrix, the information poured into it is moulded into a strategic snapshot of the business, which is then used to plot its future direction.

The first step in using the matrix is to break the company down into strategic business units (SBUs). An SBU could be a subsidiary, a division, a product or a brand – any unit with its own customers and competitors. The unit's position is plotted within the matrix according to two variables – its strength in its market, and the attractiveness of that market.

The unit's relative market share – that is, market share as a proportion of its biggest competitor – is charted on one axis. So if the SBU has 10% of a market segment and its largest rival has 40%, it has a relative market share

1920

Decentralization

of 25% (or 0.25). If the positions were reversed, it would have a relative market share of 400% (or 4.0). The growth rate of the market itself is plotted along the other axis.

Henderson chose these two variables because of their implications for cash generation and consumption. In line with his experience curve theory, an increase in relative market share should be accompanied by a cost advantage and, therefore, an increase in cash generation. A rapidly growing market demands investment in capacity, which means increased consumption of cash. These principles are reflected in the analysis that follows once the unit's position in the matrix has been established.

The business will occupy one of four quarters of the two-by-two box that is created, to be labelled, and dealt with, in one of the following ways.

Cash cows Business units with a high share of a mature (i.e. low-growth) market are called cash cows. As such, they should generate more cash than they consume. They should be milked of their cash and fed as little as possible. The cash can then be used to build up question marks and fund existing stars (see below), diversify into new businesses and pay the shareholders.

Stars Businesses are known as stars when they have a relatively strong position in a high-growth market. They generate lots of cash but, because of their own growth,

> **Pets [dogs] are not necessary. They are evidence of failure either to obtain a leadership position during the growth phase, or to get out and cut the losses.**
>
> **Bruce Henderson,** 1970

Relative market share — High / Low; Market growth — High / Low

STARS · QUESTION MARKS · CASH COWS · DOGS

More matrices

General Electric, a monolithic central planner in its day, called on the help of consultants McKinsey & Co to refine the Boston matrix, producing its own, more detailed and sophisticated version. The relative share axis is replaced by a broader 'competitive strength' measure, incorporating factors like relative brand strength, customer loyalty, distribution strength, innovation record and access to finance.

Along the other axis, market growth is elaborated into 'market attractiveness', including features such as market size and profitability, pricing trends and opportunity to differentiate. In the GE grid itself, a three-by-three structure replaces Boston's two-by-two. So the simple distinction between 'high' and 'low' share and growth becomes a distinction between 'high', 'medium' and 'low' competitive strength and market attractiveness.

they consume lots of it too. That's as it should be, and they should be given as much investment as needed to maintain their relative market share. If they do, once the market slows down they will become cash cows. If not, and they are allowed to lose share, they may become dogs.

> **All products eventually become either cash cows or pets [dogs].**
> Bruce Henderson, 1970

Dogs As the name implies, dogs combine the worst of both worlds, though Henderson originally called them 'pets'. They have a weak position in a low- or no-growth segment. While they don't consume much cash, they don't generate much either and are unlikely to be very profitable. The theory says they should be strong candidates for disposal, raising cash that can then be used to feed stars or diversify. Critics have argued that units in the doghouse – which may, after all, house many of a company's SBUs – are quite capable of being turned into cash cows.

Question marks Sometimes called 'problem children', question marks are the trickiest units to deal with. They operate in attractive, growing markets, but have low share. So, while they are consuming cash to

> **If cash is not supplied [to question marks], they fall behind and die.**
> **Bruce Henderson, 1970**

fund growth, they are not generating much. The question is which ones are worth the added investment required to grow market share and turn them into stars.

The Boston matrix set the business world alight in the early 1970s and fuelled an entire culture of centralized strategic planning, business rationalization and diversification. The oil crash and accompanying slump of the mid-1970s revealed the weaknesses in central planning and diversification, and BCG and its matrix, perhaps unfairly, took much of the blame.

As others have pointed out, growth rate is only one among many features that determine the attractiveness of a market, and relative share is only one element of competitive advantage. The matrix does not acknowledge this. It is particularly harsh on dogs, which may be helping other business units to succeed or which, if the definition of their 'market' were redrawn, might not be dogs at all.

It remains, however, a revealing prism through which to observe a business and, at the very least, is a helpful starting point for any strategic discussion. Cinema has never been quite the same since Marlon Brando exploded onto the screen. And if the Boston matrix had never been invented, the corporate world might be a very different place.

the condensed idea
Dogs, stars, cows and question marks

06 BPR

Business process reengineering (BPR) was the hot management idea of the 1990s. Enthusiasm for it has cooled, but its underlying principles still make good sense, particularly when applied to bigger, older companies that have become set in their ways.

BPR was popularized, if not exactly invented, by Michael Hammer and James Champy in their 1993 book, *Reengineering the Corporation*. Hammer liked to say that BPR was about 'reversing the Industrial Revolution'. What he meant was that, while customer wants and needs were continually shifting in the new Information Age, the way in which many companies met those needs was fixed in concrete.

Unlike total quality management (TQM) (see page 184), which tended to end at the doors of each department, BPR took a bird's-eye view of the entire business, and tried to prise open the vertical hierarchies – 'silos' or 'smokestacks' – that had developed over time. It reasoned that satisfying customer needs involved processes that spread across smokestacks, and that activities needed to be reassessed in the light of the total process.

Hammer staked out BPR's foundations in a 1990 paper called 'Reengineering work: don't automate, obliterate'. His thesis was that, instead of automating work that did not add value, companies should get rid of it. This was then worked up into a full-blown theory. Hammer and Champy defined BPR as 'the fundamental rethinking and radical redesign of business processes to achieve dramatic improvements in critical, contemporary measures of performance, such as cost, quality, service and speed'. Underpinning it was the recurring question of how to add value for the customer.

timeline

1911	1951
Scientific management	Total quality management

The right direction

The US Federal Government took to BPR in a big way. Its BPR Readiness
Assessment Guide, issued in 1996, told government agencies that the following
transitions had to take place in any reengineering approach:

Source: Government Business Process Reengineering Readiness
Assessment Guide, General Services Administration 1996

From	▶	To
Paper-driven	▶	Electronic-based
Hierarchical	▶	Networked
Power by hoarding information	▶	Power by sharing information
Stand-alone	▶	Virtual and digital
Control-oriented	▶	Performance-oriented
Compliance-oriented	▶	Benchmark-oriented
Sole resident experts	▶	Teams by talent
Stovepipe organizations	▶	Honeycombed organizations
Oversight agencies	▶	Coaching agencies
Slow response	▶	Prompt response
Data entered more than once	▶	Data entered once
Technology-fearful	▶	Technology-savvy
Decisions pushed to top of agency	▶	Decisions pushed to customer transaction

The words in the definition were carefully chosen. BPR is **fundamental**,
because it asks the questions 'why do we do this?' and 'why do we do it this
way?' People must question the old rules and assumptions.

It's **radical** because it starts with a clean sheet, disregarding existing
structures and procedures. Reengineering is not reorganizing. It's **dramatic**
because it seeks to make substantial improvements, not marginal tweaks.
Many of the companies that implemented BPR did so because they were in
serious trouble or could see that they might be one day soon.

1954	1979	1990s	1993
Management by objectives	Benchmarking	Customer relationship management	BPR

> **Some companies may eschew the term reengineering and employ other phrases, such as process redesign or transformation. But at their heart, such efforts fit our definition perfectly.**
>
> **Michael Hammer, 2003**

Processes are pivotal to BPR. Classically, organizations are divided into departments, and processes are divided into tasks that are then distributed across those departments. BPR reviews those tasks in the light of the ultimate purpose they are designed to achieve and focuses sharply on customer needs.

Hammer and Champy quote the example of IBM Credit Corporation's credit approval process, which used to take an average of six days but could last up to two weeks. During that time IBM would often lose the order to a competitor. It was a five-step process. The salesperson called in with a finance request which was written down on paper by an operator in central office. The paper went to the credit department, where the customer's credit was checked, the result noted on the paper, and the paper sent to the business practices department. The business practices department would modify the standard loan contract to suit the customer's special requests, attach any special terms to the paper, and forward the paper to the price department. The price department would decide the appropriate interest rate for the customer and add it to the paper, before sending it to administration. Administration produced a quotation letter, which went to the salesperson, who delivered it to the customer – if they still had one.

After trying a number of unsuccessful fixes, executives took a request for finance and literally walked it through the five steps. It took them one and a half hours, end to end. The problem lay not in how long people took to do the job but in the structure of the process itself and all those handovers.

Closer analysis revealed a hidden assumption that every request was unique and had to be assessed by specialists – four of them. In fact, most requests were fairly standard and could easily be handled by a generalist, as long as they were supported by a computer system that was easy to use. This use of information technology as an enabler is integral to BPR, as long as it is not used simply to automate the old tasks, and as long as the IT department is not involved in redesigning the tasks.

Hammer and Champy suggested the following BPR principles:
• organize around outcomes, not tasks;
• integrate information processing work into the real work that produces the information;

• treat geographically dispersed resources as though they were centralized – IT can help;
• link parallel workflow activities instead of just integrating their results;
• put the decision-making point where the work is performed and build control into the process;
• capture information once – at the source.

No manual There is no step-by-step manual for BPR, but common methods include combining several jobs into one, allowing workers to make decisions, minimizing reconciliation, and providing a single point of contact for the customer. Factors that could prevent BPR success include:
• trying to fix a process instead of changing it;
• trying to make it happen from the bottom up;
• settling for minor results;
• quitting too early;
• skimping on resources;
• concentrating exclusively on design;
• placing prior constraints on problem definition or scope of the effort;
• trying not to make anyone unhappy.

Apart from IBM, companies that claimed success with BPR include Procter & Gamble, General Motors and Ford. Yet up to 70% of BPR projects have failed, possibly due to some of the factors listed above.

> **While the first wave of reengineering primarily focused on back-room transactional processes ... the current wave has a much broader scope, encompassing creative work ranging from product development to marketing.**
>
> **Michael Hammer, 2003**

After its first burst of popularity, the theory was criticized for its lack of attention to the human dimension. Some called it 'the new Taylorism' (see page 152) and said it was merely an excuse for getting rid of employees. Hammer later recanted somewhat, admitting he had neglected people's values and beliefs and insisting that these should not be ignored. Subsequent and gentler, less radical versions of BPR are called business process redesign, business process improvement and business process management.

the condensed idea
A complete rethink of business processes

07 Brand

Apple has been running a transatlantic advertising campaign featuring two friends, Mac and PC. PC – he wears a tie – is nice enough but a little geeky and buttoned down. Doing what he has to, which is to be a computer, is a bit of a performance and ever-so-slightly perplexing. Mac – casual shirt – is relaxed, cool, takes everything in his stride. Not smug, he's simply the sort of guy you wouldn't mind meeting in a bar. Who would you rather have a relationship with?

The campaign, which has played around the world using well-known faces in the roles of Mac and PC, takes the next logical step in brand advertising. It does what other marketers have been urging, which is to 'humanize' the brand – except that Apple has done it literally. Brands have travelled a long way from the rear ends of Texas cattle. Like the original, marketing brands are supposed to burn an image of the product into your brain. Marketing types won't all agree on a precise definition, but it has broadened from the original 'name, mark or symbol' to something like 'the sum of all experiences and values associated with particular product, service or company'. That's not an exclusive list, since any entity that wants your money or attention nowadays is capable of building a brand, including people (Madonna, Martha Stewart), cities and countries. The top three country brands in 2006, according to the Anholt Nation Brand Index were the UK, Germany and Canada. The US came tenth.

'Name, mark or symbol' brands are coeval with packaged goods, which takes them back in essence, if not name, to the 19th century. Early 'brands' included Campbell's Soup and, of course, Coca-Cola, still the world's most valuable brand, according to consultants Interbrand. Ad man James

timeline

1886	1916	1924
Brand	Diversification	Market segmentation

Umbrella brands

The world's two biggest branded goods companies, Procter & Gamble and its European counterpart, Unilever, have traditionally stood back and let their product brands speak for themselves. But in 2004, the year before its 75th anniversary, Unilever decided to push its corporate brand to the fore. By the following year, a new Unilever logo had been stamped on every pack the group sold.

The world was changing, it said, and customers demanded more from the companies behind the brands, bringing their views as citizens into buying decisions. They wanted brands they could trust. The new Unilever brand would stand visibly behind its products, in a spirit of transparency and accountability.

Waving the Unilever logo may help flagging products, though the group has had a major brand cleanout, slashing its portfolio of brands from 1,600 to 400. Potential investors will now be reminded of the company every time they pull a jar of Hellman's off the shelf. And the company hopes for a new sense of 'Unileverness' among staff, whose loyalties have been drawn to their own brands. Does Proctor & Gamble intend to follow? No, sir. Umbrella branding forces a parent to maintain consistency among its businesses. Proctor & Gamble likes the independence of its brands.

Walter Thompson published an explanation of trademark advertising around the turn of the century, after which more companies developed a taste for symbols, mascots and slogans. When radio arrived in the 1920s, the slogans morphed into jingles. Academia began to impose order in 1955. Burleigh Gardner and Sidney Levy suggested in *The Product and the Brand* that the brand itself was less important than the customer's perception of brand. They called it 'brand image', arguing that it was an inseparable part of branding that required creation, development and management. An industry was born.

1960	1964	1970	2004
What business are you really in?	The four Ps of marketing	Corporate social responsibility	Web 2.0

Before, the mantra was to make the brand irreplaceable. That's not enough today – it has to be irresistible.

Kevin Roberts
(CEO Saatchi & Saatchi)

Still selling soup Brand managers learnt to feed those perceptions by associating their products with attractive qualities – reliability, quality, health, youthfulness, luxury. This came to be known as 'branding' and led to the received wisdom that customers buy the brand, rather than the product. This was a valuable distinction in a world where competing products were becoming increasingly similar. Some brands have enjoyed very long lives in the face of energetic competition. Apart from Coke and Campbell's (still the world's largest soup company), Heinz Tomato Ketchup, Bird's Custard, Kellogg's Corn Flakes and Gillette razors are only some of the brands that have led in their markets for over half a century.

Customers like brands because of the certainty of what they promise and because they speed up choice. While they help to build and sustain customer loyalty, they bring other strategic benefits to their owners. First, and not least, they usually allow the company to charge more and, because it raises wholesalers' and retailers' margins, this premium price makes it easier to get distribution. In the groceries market, where power has shifted from manufacturers to retailers, any such leverage is worth having.

Another benefit is available through the growing practice of 'brand stretching', 'leveraging the brand' or 'brand extension'. Here, you extend the virtues of the existing brand and its name to a new product. Yves Saint Laurent set the example for every other fashion designer when he gave his name to a range of accessories from belts to sunglasses (couturier Coco Chanel had done it with perfume in the 1920s). Mars has pushed into the ice cream market, and Procter & Gamble's Fairy Soap has given us Fairy Liquid.

This takes some, though far from all, of the risk out of launching new products and can be used to create new segments within an existing market, as British Airways did with Club Class. By reintroducing a sense of freshness and diversity, brand stretching may also help to stave off the market maturity stage of the product lifecycle (see page 90), as it has in the once-faded realms of handheld razors, for example, and bicycles.

Today brand consultants talk of the need to get the customer to deepen their relationship with a brand. Human relationships, the ones that inspire

> **It is better to be first in the mind, than to be first in the marketplace. Marketing is not a battle of products; it's a battle of perceptions.**
>
> **Al Ries and Jack Trout, 1993**

the kind of loyalty and affection marketers want, invariably have significant emotional content. So now we have 'emotional branding', which is where the humanizing comes in. Marc Gobé, consultant and author of a book on emotional branding, believes that emotions sell. Emotional branding brings new credibility and personality to a brand by connecting powerfully with people on a 'personal and holistic level'. It elevates purchases based on need to the realm of desire. Apple's iPod does just that, he believes.

Building a 'brandscape' A brand is an asset and, though intangible, it has a value. These values can make a large contribution to the total worth of the companies that own them, which accounts for the zeal with which companies try to build them up. This has given some critics a platform from which to attack the whole concept of big brands. Naomi Klein touched a nerve with her book, *No Logo*, which accused brand merchants of cocooning us in a 'brandscape'. Companies were moving their factories to the third world so that, instead of making products, they could market aspirations and images, a 'Barbie world for adults'.

Klein is not the only one who is fed up with brand obsession. Former Disney chairman Michael Eisner once called the word 'overused, sterile and unimaginative'. A reliance on brands and 'brand values' has made companies vulnerable in an unaccustomed way, as companies like Nike and Shell have found to their cost, when they were seen to have besmirched their brands (see page 47). Emotional branding is all very well but – funny things – emotions can change in a heartbeat.

the condensed idea
Shaping the customer experience

08 Channel management

We hear a lot about discontinuous change these days. It first cropped up in catastrophe theory, which may give pause for thought, but business thinkers and economists like the way it describes the quantum leap – the radical shift that makes everything look different. They also like how it (eventually) boosts growth, far more than incremental change ever does.

Some of the most powerful discontinuities of the last century or so have been the coming of the horseless carriage, powered flight, the personal computer and now, dot.com bust or no, of the Internet. The Net has forced anyone running a business to reconsider exactly how they market, sell and distribute their products. And that boils down to some serious thought about channel management.

Distribution Channels are a business's routes to market, part of the 'place' in the four Ps of marketing (see page 88). In considering the four Ps, managers must make decisions on how many levels of distribution to employ. Can the firm afford – or does it even want – its own direct sales force? Will it distribute via retailers, or wholesalers and retailers, and how selectively will they be chosen?

A direct sales force is expensive but has the virtue of being firmly under the company's control. Wholesalers and retailers are not, and motivating them to do their best for you makes up a large part of traditional channel

timeline

1950	early 1950s
Supply chain management	Channel management

management. The most widely used and probably the most effective incentive is to grease their palms, either by offering more generous margins for pushing your product instead of your rivals', or by staging some form of competition to reward salespeople who do likewise. Providing them with training and the tools they need to sell the product effectively also helps.

In a vertically integrated organization, the manufacturer or supplier might own its retail outlets, or the store group might make the products that it sells – forward or backward integration, respectively. This model is inflexible, imposes high fixed costs and can be distracting for management but, like a direct sales force, it is under the company's control.

One distribution channel that gives control at low cost is mail order. And now, of course, there is the Net (a kind of mail order plus). Like most advances in technology, there were a few enthusiastic early adopters, while many sat back to wait and see. Now, however, the Net has become an indispensable channel for the majority of consumer industries and, at the very least, a marketing tool for many business-to-business firms.

> **As a result of proliferating channels, sales and marketing executives in a wide range of industries have lost control of their customers, with damaging financial consequences.**
>
> **Joseph Myers, Andrew Pickersgill and Evan van Metre, 2004** (McKinsey & Company)

Customer choice More significantly, perhaps, the Internet is not just another single channel from which to choose. Its arrival has accelerated the development of multiple-channel distribution in which customers may use different channels at different stages in the process of buying something. They might check online that an item is in stock before going into a store to buy the goods. Or they might order online for collection at the store. They might want to be able to transact by phone, online or in person on different occasions of their own choice.

1964	**1990s**	**2004**
The four Ps of marketing	Customer relationship management	Web 2.0

channel challenges

All is not what it may seem in the contemporary world of channels. Automation and the Web appear to offer cost and convenience advantages in channel management, but it's not always so.

Banks discovered as much in the late 1990s, when they fell in love with the machine. The strategy was to move transactions out of the branch and onto ATMs. The costs per transaction were lower, and staff could be more usefully employed or bid farewell. Better yet, the branch could be closed and the property sold.

To encourage this, counter staff were reduced, and queues allowed to lengthen. One UK bank levied a £1 fee for every face-to-face transaction, and many customers started to use the ATMs. But while they had banked inside the branch, say, once a week, they were enjoying the convenience and speed of the ATM two, three, four times a week – and total transaction costs actually went up. Still, at the £1-a-go bank, so many people insisted on retaining human contact, that it made £25m in extraordinary profit.

In this world of 'bricks and clicks', channel management takes on new meaning. More and more customers want, or have been persuaded to want, access to goods and information via new channels such as the Internet, the phone and – particularly in the case of financial services (an early adopter of the new channels) – the automated teller machine or ATM. As banks discovered early on, they still want the old bricks and mortar too.

Companies are spending considerable sums to oblige. Some have noticed that the customers who want multiple channels tend to have more money than the ones who only use one channel, and that they are likely to spend more too. The customers are looking for more convenience – shopping from home – and quicker access to information. The result is that multiple channels are becoming less of an opportunity for competitive advantage and more of a strategic necessity.

Managing them has its problems, however. One is what consultants call the '3E trap' – the unprofitable temptation to provide 'everything to everyone, everywhere'. The answer is, first, to know who your most profitable customers are, an area where channel management becomes intertwined with customer relationship management, or CRM (see page 56). Then, decide which channels they prefer to use.

CRM persuades us to focus on the customer, to provide a seamless, homogenous service. If multiple-channel distribution is to deliver that experience for the customer, then it has to be joined up. The channels must be managed as an interdependent, linked and coordinated system instead of as standalone operations. Some consultants call this a 'multichannel', as opposed to a multiple channel, strategy.

> **Divesting or closing stores is often part of the multi-channel solution.**
>
> **Corey Yulinsky, 2000**
> (McKinsey & Company)

No *laissez faire* The preferences of high-value customers should obviously influence how that strategy is implemented. But that's not to say that the organization should be completely passive and leave customers to use whichever channels they please. Some are more costly than others, sometimes surprisingly so (see box). Channel economics have to be understood and customers nudged in the direction of the most appropriate and, indeed, cost-effective channel.

Migrating customers to new channels is a sensitive and risky affair, so a delicate touch is needed. If that's true for customers, it can also be true for existing channels. Retailers can feel threatened by the introduction of a new and, they might believe, competing channel. Some firms have devised incentives to keep their retailers on side while they roll out new web- or phone-based sales initiatives.

Done right, the multi-channel approach can be a source of differentiation that is hard to copy. If channel management was getting humdrum before the advent of the Net, it's a lot more lively now.

the condensed idea
Routes to the customer

09 Core competence

Michael Porter and his five forces of competition looked out across the corporate battlements to survey the competitive landscape beyond. Gary Hamel and C.K. Prahalad looked within, in search of the 'core competencies' that they argued were the true source of competitive advantage. It was time, they said, for top executives to rethink the concept of the corporation.

> **'Core competencies are the wellspring of new business development.'**
>
> **Gary Hamel and C.K. Prahalad, 1990**

Hamel and Prahalad were reacting against the decentralized business portfolio strategy being followed by many large corporations. Instead of a portfolio of businesses, housed in more or less standalone 'strategic business units' (SBUs), companies should think of themselves as a portfolio of competences, they urged in a highly influential 1990 *Harvard Business Review* article, 'The core competence of the corporation'.

The industrial backdrop against which they were writing was one in which Western companies had begun to steady themselves against the low cost and high quality of Japanese imports. But now their Japanese competitors were outflanking them with wave upon wave of new products in new markets. Honda had invented the four-wheel off-road buggy and Yamaha the digital piano. Sony was cutting a swathe with its 8 mm camcorder. In the automobile market Japanese manufacturers were leading the way with in-car navigation systems and electronic engine management systems. They were maintaining their cost and quality standards, but Western companies were catching up in this department, so these were less compelling sources of competitive advantage than they had been. The

timeline

1450	1920
Innovation	Decentralization

problem in many Western companies was not that they had worse management or less technical capability than the Japanese, Hamel and Prahalad insisted. It was that their top management lacked the vision to exploit the deep reservoirs of technological capability which they undoubtedly possessed.

A core competence is something that you do better than anyone else. Indeed, the large companies at which this theory is directed should be doing it to world-class standards. It produces a core product or an efficiency, which is not an end product, but is a vital component of a range of end products. Black & Decker's core competence is making small electric motors, for example. These sit at the heart of a wide range of end products, from chain saws and lawnmowers to vacuum cleaners and automatic can openers. Canon has core competencies in optics and precision mechanics, which it transferred hugely successfully from cameras to copiers and now laser printers. Honda's core competence is in engines and power trains, which gives it an advantage in making and selling cars, motorcycles, tractor mowers and generators. 3M is world class at stickiness.

Test of competence So core competencies open the way to many different markets. And as companies think about how to exploit these competencies, they are more likely to come up with innovations. Hamel and Prahalad laid down three tests to identify a core competence:
• it provides potential access to a wide variety of markets;
• it makes a significant contribution to perceived customer benefits of the end product;
• it is difficult to imitate.

Being world class at making a rather ordinary component, something that many others produce, will not bestow competitive advantage. A core competence makes a disproportionate contribution to customer value and must be judged relative to the competition. It should be something your competitors wish they had. It is not about outspending your rivals in

> **The future is not what will happen; the future is what is happening.**
> **Gary Hamel and C.K. Prahalad, 1996**

1960	1965	1980	1981	1990
Strategic alliances	Corporate strategy	The five forces of competition	Japanese management	Core competence

research and development. (One of the distinguishing practices of innovative Japanese manufacturers was the way in which they formed strategic alliances to obtain technologies or competencies they lacked.) It is not about shared costs between SBUs – they may be a result, but they shouldn't be a reason. And it is not about vertical integration though, again, some degree of vertical integration may result.

A firm is unlikely to have more than five or six basic competencies. If its list contains 20 items, it hasn't got the definition quite right. Companies can lose core competencies unknowingly in the name of cutting cost. Hamel and Prahalad saw how Chrysler regarded engines and power trains as just another component, which it often outsourced. They found it hard to imagine Honda surrendering manufacturing and design responsibility for so critical a part of a car's function. 'Outsourcing can provide a short cut to

Pain and gain

A painful contrast in the progress of two electronics firms with different strategic ideas was used by Hamel and Prahalad as a live example of their ideas on core competence. In the early 1980s, America's GTE looked set to become a major player in the evolving IT industry, with its substantial presence in telecoms, semiconductors, TV manufacture and display technology. NEC of Japan had a similar base, including computer manufacture, but was less than half the size.

NEC, anticipating the convergence of computers and communications, had adopted its 'C&C' strategy in 1977. It decided that success required certain competencies, especially in semiconductors, and formed over 100 alliances to build its skills quickly

and cheaply. A C&C committee oversaw the development of core products and competencies. The decentralized GTE found it hard to focus on core competencies. It did a lot of work on identifying key technologies for the coming era, but line managers continued to behave independently.

NEC went on to become the world leader in semiconductors, consolidating its position in computers and building a strong new presence in telecoms products, introducing mobile phones, laptops and fax machines, and overtaking GTE's sales by the mid-1980s. GTE abandoned semiconductor and TV production, and by the 1990s was little more than a phone company. It was bought by Bell Atlantic in 2000 to form Verizon.

a more competitive product,' they observed, 'but it typically contributes little to building the people-embodied skills that are needed to retain product leadership.'

Hamel and Prahalad saw decentralization and 'the tyranny of the SBU' as the enemy of core competence. In an organization made up of many SBUs, no single unit may feel responsible for nurturing core competence. SBUs tend to be locked in the present, concentrating on maximizing today's sales. While they may have built up competencies, they are often inclined to hoard them, and may be reluctant to lend talented people to another SBU to pursue new opportunities. If core competence is not shared or recognized, innovations flowing from SBUs will tend to be incremental.

> **The benefits of competencies, like . . . money supply, depend on the velocity of their circulation.**
> **Gary Hamel and C.K. Prahalad, 1990**

Architects of the future Management's job, therefore, is to develop an organization-wide 'strategic architecture', a road map of the future that identifies which competencies to build and what technologies they need. Core competencies should become corporate resources and SBUs should have to bid for them just as they have to bid for capital resources. Reward systems and career paths should break out of SBU silos and key employees should be weaned off the idea that they belong to one particular business. Interestingly, one of the main planks of Jack Welch's famous General Electric makeover, well under way by this time, was the idea of the 'boundaryless company'.

The diversified corporation, according to Hamel and Prahalad, is a large tree, with trunk and limbs as its core products, the smaller (SBUs, please note) branches as business units and the leaves, flowers and fruit as the end products. The root system that nourishes, sustains and stabilizes is the core competence. If you look only at the leaves of a tree, they said, you won't notice its strength. In the same way, you may fail to see the strength of competitors if you look only at their end products.

the condensed idea
The roots of competitive advantage

10 Corporate governance

America was treated to a peep at the CEO's expense account recently, to discover, among other things, that the boss of American Express was paid $132,000 for personal use of company cars and reimbursed for snacks from the company dining room. Some people were more upset by the snacks than by the car. More of this kind of information is being made public because the US Securities & Exchange Commission has lowered the threshold for disclosure of perks. But executive pay and disclosure are only two of an increasing number of management activities subject to the stern eye of 'corporate governance'.

Because of the agency problem, shareholders have fretted over good governance for many years. They want to be fairly treated and given a hearing, particularly where there is a big majority shareholder that doesn't always listen to what the 'minorities' want. Ruling cliques or family interests sometimes give themselves more voting power by issuing different classes of shares – where A shares have two votes for every B share, for example, and guess who's got the A shares? Shareholders want to know what's going on inside the company, how management is spending 'their' money and how reckless or wise its plans may be. So they are always pushing for more disclosure. The ultimate cockpit of decision-making is the boardroom, so shareholders also take a keen interest in how boards are structured, who the directors are and how trammelled or otherwise is the CEO's power.

timeline

1916
Diversification

1938
Leadership

Governments have traditionally taken less interest in the minutiae of corporate governance, apart from ensuring that directors didn't break the law and companies didn't behave in a monopolistic fashion. In the UK it was private-sector concerns about corporate governance, fuelled by the BCCI and Robert Maxwell fraud cases, that prompted a series of investigations into financial reporting, director's pay, governance and the role of non-executive directors. Most of the important recommendations were bundled into the Combined Code in 1998. Though government commissioned the last report, the Code remains voluntary. About half of the companies listed on the London Stock Exchange comply, though the exchange insists that those who don't must explain why in their annual reports.

> **❛Good corporate governance should provide incentives for the board and management to pursue objectives that are in the interest of the company and its shareholders.❜**
>
> **OECD, 2004**

Better boards One of the Code's recommendations is that the chairman should be 'independent', not from within the company and certainly not the ex-CEO. Nor should the chairman and the CEO be the same person, because that's too much concentration of power. The board should be evenly balanced between non-executives – who are less under the CEO's sway and more likely to ask the searching questions – and executives, who know the business. A remuneration committee should decide on directors' pay, an audit committee should deal with the auditors, and only non-executives should sit on both. The Code has served as a model for similar codes in a number of continental European countries.

The outbreak of corporate scandal disease – Enron, WorldCom, Tyco *et al.* – that tore through corporate America in 2002, made the US government finally sit bolt upright. Its response was swift and uncompromising – the Sarbanes-Oxley Act. This set up the Public Company Accounting Oversight Board to keep a beady eye on auditors, and made independent audit committees compulsory for listed firms. It obliged CEOs and chief financial officers to certify the company's accounts and promised to send

1970	**1984**	**1998**
Corporate social responsibility	Stakeholders	Corporate governance

Pointers of principle

'The integrity of businesses and markets is central to the vitality and stability of our economies.' So says the 30-member OECD, insisting that good corporate governance contributes to growth and financial stability. The *OECD Principles of Good Governance*, guidance for governments rather than companies, were issued in 1999 and updated in 2004:

1. Ensuring the basis for an effective corporate governance framework – the corporate governance framework (CGF) should promote transparent and efficient markets, be consistent with the rule of law and clearly articulate the division of responsibilities among different supervisory, regulatory and enforcement authorities.

2. The rights of shareholders and key ownership functions – the CGF should protect and facilitate the exercise of shareholders' rights.

3. The equitable treatment of shareholders – the CGF should ensure the equitable treatment of all shareholders, including minority and foreign shareholders. All shareholders should have the opportunity to obtain effective redress for violation of their rights.

4. The role of stakeholders in corporate governance – the CGF should recognize the rights of stakeholders established by law or through mutual agreements and encourage active cooperation between corporations and stakeholders in creating wealth, jobs and the sustainability of financially sound enterprises.

5. Disclosure and transparency - the CGF should ensure that timely and accurate disclosure is made on all material matters regarding the corporation, including the financial situation, performance, ownership and governance of the company.

6. The responsibilities of the board – the CGF should ensure the strategic guidance of the company, the effective monitoring of management by the board, and the board's accountability to the company and the shareholders.

them to jail if these proved false. UK boards have been moving towards the Combined Code model for some years, with some notable exceptions, such as HSBC. In America, the absolute monarchy of the CEO (usually the chairman as well) remains in relative good health though there is an observable shift in power towards the directors. There is also less 'I serve on your board and you serve on mine'. Indeed, as compliance burdens rise, the dwindling number of CEOs and executive directors willing to serve on other companies' boards is noticeable on both sides of the Atlantic. In the

UK, serving directors are more inclined to accept directorships in private-equity-owned companies, away from the spotlight.

Change in Japan Corporate governance is overwhelmingly an Anglo-American preoccupation, though one that is spreading across the rest of Europe. Some change is taking place in the Japanese system, as firms respond to pressures from foreign investors. Japanese boards have always been big, and closed to anything resembling an independent director. Some are now taking on one or two outside directors and shrinking in size. Western thinking is that smaller boards allow serious discussion but, if there are many more than a dozen members, matters tend to get waved through.

> **CEOs stocked their boards with CEOs they knew as a way of decreasing the possibility for dissent.**
> **Patrick McGurn,** 2007
> (Institutional Shareholder Services, ISS)

In an effort to spread the word more widely, the Organisation for Economic Cooperation and Development (OECD) has laid down corporate governance principles for its member states. As it points out, good practice nowadays will boost a company's share price and, by leading to better credit ratings, can mean cheaper debt. A Harvard/Wharton study showed that US firms with better governance had faster sales growth and were more profitable than their peer groups. But most agree that there is no single model for good corporate governance. Even in a world dominated by multinationals, it is difficult to export a corporate governance system, rooted as they are in domestic laws and habits.

So things have swung the shareholder's way in recent years. Investors have more influence over management than they have ever had. Of course, it's never quite enough for them. They still think CEOs get paid too much, even though a good one will repay his package many times over. And they would just love to have more say in the selection of directors who, they believe, should be able to hire and fire management. So far, management has held them off on that one.

the condensed idea
More demanding standards of behaviour

11 Corporate social responsiblilty

Economist Milton Friedman and *The Economist* news magazine are only two of the parties who have taken a dim view of 'corporate social responsibility' (CSR). Friedman said in 1970 that the social responsibility of business was to increase its profits. *The Economist* called it woolly and dangerous thinking and published a two-by-two matrix to explain what that meant. Yet even companies that agree may eventually have to come to terms with it.

The Economist plotted CSR's effect on profits against its effect on social welfare. If CSR raised social welfare while reducing profits, it was nothing but 'borrowed virtue', the magazine grumbled, doing good at the expense of shareholders. If it grew profits while reducing social welfare, it was pernicious and if it reduced both, it was nothing short of delusional. If, however, CSR produced a win–win increase in social welfare and profits at the same time, well, that wasn't CSR – it was simply good management.

The magazine argued that business should not try to do the work of governments, and vice versa, which is a fair point. But given the preoccupations of a growing slice of society, 'social welfare' is a rather narrow proxy for CSR which, by any current definition, now embraces sustainable development and environmental responsibility.

The view in an old-fashioned boardroom, echoing *The Economist*, may well be that CSR is little more than a begging bowl, to be fed, at best, by

timeline

1886
Brand

1938
Leadership

sponsoring the chairman's hobbies or his wife's charities. But the times are a-changing. In the wake of recurring accounting scandals and environmental disasters, the public mood is demanding more of corporate standards of behaviour, and mood can have a hard edge. Whether managers believe CSR is within their jurisdiction or not, they have to make decisions based on the facts and, as Alfred P. Sloan would say, opinions in the marketplace are facts.

> **'Corporate social responsibility is a hard-edged business decision. Not because it is a nice thing to do or because people are forcing us to do it ... because it is good for our business.'**
>
> **Niall Fitzgerald, 2003**
> (former CEO, Unilever)

What exactly is CSR? There is no single definition. The World Business Council for Sustainable Development says it's 'the continuing commitment by business to behave ethically and contribute to economic development while improving the quality of life of the workforce and their families as well as of the local community and society at large.' More succinctly, Mallen Baker of the UK's Business in the Community says it's 'about how companies manage the business processes to produce an overall positive impact on society'.

Europe vs US CSR's cheerleaders are not helped by it meaning one thing in the UK and Europe, and another in the US. The European perception is more inclusive, seeing CSR as honest and considerate behaviour that makes a positive attempt to leave the world a better place. In America, the idea of the 'good corporate citizen' is split in two. The closest equivalent to Europe's CSR is 'business ethics', which is more about keeping your nose clean and upholding moral standards. CSR is straight charity or philanthropy, a way of saying thank you for the profits without expecting anything in return – if you did, it wouldn't be philanthropic.

Taking the broader view, CSR covers a multitude of sins, literally. The Global Reporting Initiative, which provides a framework for companies to report on their CSR compliance, has 32 different performance indicators, ranging from customer privacy and anti-competitive behaviour to child

1970
Corporate social responsibility

1984
Stakeholders

1998
Corporate governance

labour and indigenous rights. The prospect of adding to their existing compliance reporting burden – groan – still blunts some companies' enthusiasm for CSR. Institutional investors are increasingly alert to the issue, however, and more are asking companies to prove their CSR credentials. Ethical investment is showing that it can outperform more general benchmarks, and it is the effect on the share price that may eventually win over the Friedmanite camp.

Licence to operate CSR proponents argue that this is not about giving away money that rightfully belongs to the shareholders. They say it is about sustaining a business's licence to operate, by managing its relationships with influential constituencies – customers, staff, the community at large. CSR means managing your risk and your reputation.

Ethics, what ethics?

Consumers don't think much of companies' ethics and, according to a five-country survey, are turning to 'ethical consumerism'. Germany saw least to celebrate, with 64% of respondents perceiving a deterioration in standards. The US was next, with 55%. Nearly half of the consumers who were asked in the UK, France and Spain also thought that ethical behaviour had grown worse. UK shoppers emerged as the most critical, and Spaniards the most sceptical about ethical 'hype'. None the less, the survey's ranking of most ethically perceived brands contains one or two surprises:

UK	US	FRANCE	GERMANY	SPAIN
1 Co-op (incl. Co-op Bank)	Coca-Cola	Danone	Adidas	Nestlé
2 Body Shop	Kraft	Adidas Nike	Nike Puma	Body Shop
3 Marks & Spencer	Procter & Gamble			Coca-Cola
4 Traidcraft	Johnson & Johnson Kellogg's Nike Sony	Nestlé	BMW	Danone
5 Cafédirect Ecover		Renault	Demeter gepa	Corte Inglés

Source: GfK NOP 2007

There are statistics that purport to show the beneficial impact of CSR on a company's bottom line, but they are not yet overwhelmingly convincing. It's easier to prove the cost of neglect, with mounting examples of the cost of reputational damage from negative CSR. Most quoted is Brent Spar, a North Sea oil platform that had reached the end of its life. Owner Shell decided that sinking it at sea was the most environmentally responsible option and perhaps it was. But the public, orchestrated by Greenpeace activists, decided otherwise. The outcry and ensuing boycott of Shell products forced the company to back down. Shell, past masters of thinking about the future, had science on its side, but Greenpeace armed itself with values. Values won.

> **It takes 20 years to build a reputation and five minutes to ruin it.**
> **Warren Buffet**
> (Chairman, Berkshire Hathaway)

Footwear mogul Nike is still dealing with the backlash of a UK-instigated campaign that accused it of employing child labour in developing countries. It responded proactively with a rigorous CSR initiative, including the appointment of a director of sustainable development. In many markets, its reputation has been restored. In a recent survey of most 'ethical' brands by country (see box), however, Nike did not appear anywhere in the UK ranking.

Climate change is the *issue du jour* in many Western markets, and could drive home the power of public sentiment. The largest UK advertising agencies predict a wave of green marketing campaigns as businesses rush to brandish their environmental credentials. They believe consumers will punish companies not seen to be green.

Tomorrow's World, a pro-CSR business lobby, fears that CSR could go one of two ways. In one future, it would be an expression of values, with companies free to say they cared only for shareholders, but with the market seeing clearly where organizations stood. That would be 'conviction CSR'. In the other, social pressures would force compliance and companies would win applause for saying the right things in their reports – 'compliance CSR'. The consumer would surely be able to sniff out which was which.

the condensed idea
Managing risk and reputation

12 Corporate strategy

Strategy is sexy. It's the alpha male of business functions, the one to which all others – manufacturing, operations, marketing, finance, accounting, human resources *et al*. – bend the knee. Young management consultants want to be strategy consultants when they grow up, and who can blame them? Strategy is the architect (objectives, perhaps, are the client) and what follows are the hard hats. But if it looks sexy from afar, up close it can be demanding toil, and as many companies misconceive or misapprehend it as make it work.

Strategy is as old as war which, if you look in a dictionary, still crops up before business in any definition. 'The art of war' neatly sums up its military application, but management writers' definitions are seldom as short. Gerry Johnson and Kevan Scholes, in their *Exploring Corporate Strategy*, offer: 'Strategy is the direction and scope of an organization over the long-term: which achieves advantage for the organization through its configuration of resources within a challenging environment, to meet the needs of markets and to fulfil stakeholder expectations.' Michael Porter is more succinct, and comes from a different angle: 'Strategy has to do with what will make you unique', he told an audience at the Wharton School recently.

> **'Strategy is about winning.'**
> **Robert M. Grant, 1995**

However you define it, strategy wasn't a deliberate preoccupation of managers for many years. They thought and planned, and some tried to be different, but that was just part of running the business and wasn't

timeline

500BC	AD1450
War and strategy	Innovation

Mission incredible

The mission statement is now a much-loved adornment of the annual report. Some are sententious to the point of self-delusion. Dilbert.com, virtual home of the cartoon company geek, has a mission statement generator which spews out randomly constructed but all-too-familiar examples: *'We strive to assertively enhance mission-critical intellectual capital in order to completely leverage existing error-free catalysts for change while promoting personal employee growth.'*

Properly thought through, however, mission statements can serve as a valuable touchstone for management and employees, helping to keep the company's values and culture aligned, alive and well. They generally combine three things:

• our mission – our purpose, why we're in business;
• our values – our style, what is unchanging and important about the way we work;
• our vision – our goals, where we want to be in X years.

The mission statement doesn't – shouldn't – create mission and values, but instead simply expresses what already exists. Brainstorming the mission statement might reveal a purpose or style that has never been properly articulated, but they should reflect the truth and not some Dilbert-like aspiration. Aspiration belongs in the vision, which could be a target or a transformation of some kind. A mission statement is not, not ever, a strategy.

crystallized as 'strategy' much before the 1950s. Then, in 1965, H. Igor Ansoff published his *Corporate Strategy*, which brought the topic together with 'strategic management' – its formulation and implementation – to a much wider corporate audience.

A rule for making decisions Acknowledged as the father of strategic management, Ansoff said that strategy was 'a rule for making decisions', and few would argue with that. He distinguished between

1916	1960	1965	1968	1980	1990	2004
Diversification	Strategic alliances	Corporate strategy	Boston matrix	The five forces of competition	Core competence	Blue ocean strategy

objectives, which set the goals, and strategy, which set the path to the goals. And he believed firmly that 'structure follows strategy'. Strategic decisions had to answer three fundamental questions:
• What are the firm's objectives and goals?
• Should the firm diversify and, if so, into what and how vigorously?
• How should the firm develop and exploit its present product–market position?

He flagged up an important issue that has bedevilled strategy formulation ever since, which is that most decisions are made inside a framework of limited resources. No matter how big or small the company, strategic decisions mean making choices between alternative resource commitments. Grow the existing business and forget diversification? Diversify and risk neglecting the existing business? 'The object is to produce a resource-allocation pattern which will offer the best potential for meeting the firm's objectives', he says, and then shows how to do it.

> **'Policy is a contingent decision, where strategy is a rule for making decisions.'**
>
> **H. Igor Ansoff, 1985**

Ansoff set off an explosion in strategic planning, and soon everybody who was anybody had set up a corporate planning department that spun out sheaves of Soviet-style five-year forecasts and targets. While their day soon passed and Ansoff's own ideas became less prescriptive ('analysis is paralysis' – he said it first), later thinkers still have a lot to thank him for. For those who don't indulge in tomes on theory, he is best remembered for Ansoff's product–market matrix, a still-useful tool for deciding, strategically, how to expand the business. Its four possible strategies use different combinations of products and markets: **market penetration**, the safest strategy, is growing share of an existing market with an existing product; **product development** is selling new products to existing customers; **market development** is finding new customers for existing products; and **diversification**, the riskiest, is finding new markets for new products.

Planning pipeline The corporate planning department may have folded its tent, but strategic planning remains an indispensable function. The process typically unfolds in this order:
• Mission statement and objectives – describe the company's vision and define measurable financial and strategic objectives.
• Environmental scanning – gather internal and external information and

analyse the firm, its industry and the wider environment. Stamping ground of the 'five forces' (see page 84) and SWOT (strengths, weaknesses, opportunities, threats) analysis.

• Strategy formulation – the hard part. Off-the-shelf 'competitive advantage', 'core competence', or do you really think from the inside out?
• Strategy implementation – the next hard part. Communicating the strategy, organizing resources and motivating the people to deliver it.
• Evaluation and control – measure, compare with the plan and adjust.

Finding a 'right' or even a 'good' strategy is, of course, another matter entirely, though there is plenty of willing advice on hand. Michael Porter thinks head-on competition is a mistake. He says no one wins that sort of struggle, which often comes from setting out to be the 'best' in the industry. 'Best' is in the eye of the beholder. Better is to develop strategy around your unique place in the market.

Porter is also dismissive of shareholder value as a corporate goal and calls it the Bermuda Triangle of strategy: 'Shareholder value is a result. Shareholder value comes from creating superior economic performance.' Operational effectiveness is not strategy but an extension of best practice. That can be good for performance, but hard to sustain – if it's best practice, others will do it too.

Richard Koch (see page 70) thinks that corporate strategy's account may be operating in the red, and that over the last half century it has done more harm than good. This is not because it is a bad thing, but because it is invariably run from what he calls – and you can almost feel his lips tighten – 'the Centre'. Most, though not all, Centres destroy more value than they create. They can be good at sorting out financial crises, identifying turning points, finding appropriate acquisitions and integrating them, and at carrying out some Boston matrix-style (see page 20) portfolio management. Apart from those, Koch says, strategy should be left to the business units.

> **❝Strategy is the great work of the organization.❞**
>
> **Sun Tzu, c.500 BC**

the condensed idea
How to get there

13 Costs of complexity

The customer rules. If businesses have learnt anything in the last 50 years, it's to stay laser-focused on the customers and their needs. Give them innovation, give them choice, right? Well, up to a point. Some of those businesses have twigged that rich novelty and variety leads to complexity, and that complexity costs.

Keep it simple. This is not a new idea. Its most famous advocate, though not its first, was the English Franciscan friar, William of Occam. 'Occam's razor' said, essentially, that the simplest solution was usually the best, and that was in the 14th century. Sadly, Occam is silent on the profit implications of his principle. Rather more recently, however, consultants Bain & Company found that the 'lowest complexity' companies grew revenues nearly twice as fast as their peers, among the group of 75 it studied across a dozen different industries. It added that revenue growth appeared far more closely linked to levels of complexity than to company size.

> **'Complexity accumulates over time.'**
> **Eric Clemons, 2006**
> (Wharton School)

The more complex a business becomes, the higher its costs. Added complexity may come from many different directions, often associated with expanding the business in some way. It may arise as a result of innovation, extending the product line, or adding new customers. Adopting new technologies and skills adds complexity almost by definition. This kind of market-driven complexity may pay for itself, but the business needs to allocate and determine the added costs correctly

timeline

14th century	1897
Costs of complexity	Mergers and acquisitions

(see box) in order to decide. It may discover that the benefits of expansion are less than it anticipated or, indeed, may even be negative.

More machine time One consultant tells of a packaged food company that tried to defend its market share through an aggressive innovation programme. The more it added to its product line, however, the more costs mounted. The marketing team had to be increased by 20%, and inventory levels shot up. On the factory floor, over 30% of available machine time was taken up by changeovers for yet another product. To compensate, the company did longer runs of the low-volume

Learn your ABC

A true picture of the costs of complexity relies on the ability to pinpoint where they arise, product by product, particularly when it comes to indirect costs like administration and marketing. Traditional accounting methods are not much help here, because they allocate indirect costs to each product in proportion to its direct labour and materials cost. Yet apparently similar products may actually have significantly different costs, say because one spends more time on the machine, involves more administration or takes longer to sell. If so, it is subsidizing the others.

Robert S. Kaplan (see page 8) and William Bruns came to the rescue in 1987 with 'activity-based costing' (ABC). This traces indirect costs back to individual products, and can be used in service firms as well as manufacturing. It identifies 'cost drivers' and assigns costs to them, based on the number of activities they involve and the time they take.

As well as attaching costs more accurately to the products or services that incur them, ABC can identify the firm's most and least profitable customers, and gives management a more realistic picture of where problems are occurring. It doesn't conform to general accounting standards, however, and can only be used internally. So some companies don't use ABC because they balk at having to generate two different sets of accounts.

1924	1950	1985	1993
Market segmentation	Supply chain management	Value chain	BPR

> **Pluralitas non est ponenda sine necessitate (or "don't complicate unless you have to").**
>
> William of Occam, c.1285–1349

items – which then grew stale before they got to the consumer. The company's innovation strategy, by means of the additional complexity associated with it, threatened to wipe out its cost position, not to mention its market franchise.

Complexity creeps in beneath other disguises. Mergers and acquisitions can deliver all kinds of complexity (see page 136). An overlarge portfolio of businesses may distract attention from the core activities. Complexity may be too many suppliers or keeping in-house a process that could be more efficiently or effectively outsourced. Fiddly, complicated product designs or process flows add complexity and cost. More levels of hierarchical management equals more complexity. Writer and former strategy consultant Richard Koch believes that about half of all the value-added costs in the average company are complexity-related, and that half of that half offer opportunities for radical cost reduction. 'Waging war on complexity can lead simultaneously to stunning cost reductions and improvements in customer value', he says.

In their 2004 book, *Conquering Complexity in Your Business*, consultants Michael George and Stephen Wisdom offer three simple maxims:
• eliminate complexity that customers will not pay for;
• exploit the complexity that customers will pay for;
• minimize the costs of the complexity you offer.

George and Wisdom note that the most common situation is for companies to carry more products and services than their customers really want. Getting rid of some not only removes a source of unnecessary costs – *muda*, or 'waste', as the Japanese would say – but can also lead to competitive advantage. They point to low-cost carrier Southwest Airlines, which remains competitive in a commoditized industry, partly because of its low costs and unique culture, but also thanks to low complexity. This was designed in when it chose to operate only one type of aircraft – the Boeing 737. American Airlines, by contrast, historically operated up to 14 types, with 14 spares depots, 14 kinds of mechanic and pilot training, 14 different FAA certifications, none of which adds value for the customer and none of which the customer wants to pay for. American, to be fair, has since latched onto this and has been rationalizing its fleet.

Dealing with complexity needn't mean getting rid of it. Just make sure you charge for it. Baskin-Robbins has over 1000 different ice cream flavours, which is fairly complex, but customers pay a premium for them. Conquering complexity, George and Wisdom say, is either to have a very low level of it in the marketplace, or to target customers who are willing to pay an adequate premium for higher complexity delivered at a low cost.

> **'The cost of complexity isn't offset by what you can charge.'**
> **Gerard Arpey,** 2003
> (CEO American Airlines)

Find the fulcrum Bain's Mark Gottfredson maintains that cutting complexity can raise revenues as well as reduce costs, but that slashing it to zero is clearly not the right answer. Henry Ford made that mistake, producing black cars only. General Motors came along, added colours (and complexity), and overtook Ford as market leader – a position Ford has never recovered. All the same, most companies have not found their 'innovation fulcrum', Gottfredson says. 'That's the point where products or services fully meet customer needs with the lowest possible complexity costs.' He advocates choosing one average product for the company and asking what costs would be if it made only that. Do research into what kinds of complexity customers really value, and then add them back one at a time – for as long as the customer is prepared to pay what it costs to add them back.

The innovation fulcrum should be fairly easy to spot. Rationalizing product lines can get more best-selling products on retail display, raising sales. 'Let's say you have 17,000 SKUs [stock keeping units] in your catalogue, but your average retailer is carrying only 17. What's the probability that the right 17 will be there?'

Eric Clemons, Wharton professor of operations and information management, also advocates finding a balance. 'Complexity management isn't the same as cost management', he points out. 'It's about giving every customer exactly what he wants without your cost structure killing you.'

the condensed idea
Keep it simple

14 Customer relationship management

Some ideas continue to command respect among hardened management theorists years after they first appeared, and some provoke snorts of derision. Customer relationship management or CRM – around which an entire industry has been erected – gets more than its fair share of snorts.

We all experience CRM, the bad side of it, every time we get stuck in touch-tone hell, with a recorded voice asking us to 'please select one of the following options' – for the fifth time. Yet the underlying idea is perfectly logical – concentrate on your customers, learn about their needs and behaviour, use what you learn to improve the relationship and, ultimately, sell them more of what it is you're selling them.

> **CRM is more business philosophy than software, more passion than project.**
> **Made2Manage Systems, 2006**

Technology Big firms have used technology to do much of this, to capture and store customer information, to analyse it and to automate their sales and support teams. CRM has become very closely identified with technology as a result – indeed, 'CRM companies' are invariably software vendors. When CRM projects fail (as big IT projects so often do) or are poorly implemented, it chips away at CRM's reputation. And after some well-publicized and

timeline

Stop the bombing

CRM projects bomb at least as often as they succeed. Why? Some answer it's because companies don't understand that it's not a 'solution', but a business culture. IT provider CGI offers the top ten reasons why CRM projects fail:

1. CRM initiatives launched without a strategy.

2. The CRM strategy is not integral to the business strategy.

3. The CRM toolset is based on someone else's success.

4. CRM is launched with no regard for enterprise or customer.

5. CRM is launched without customer input.

6. CRM is considered an IT project – not business initiatives leveraging technology.

7. CRM is launched without defined metrics and objectives.

8. CRM is considered a one-time event.

9. Assuming you have a customer-centric culture because you have customers.

10. No top down leadership and employee buy-in for CRM.

CGI's definition of CRM is 'a strategic approach that combines the business processes, technology, employees, and information across an enterprise to attract and retain profitable customers.'

expensive project cancellations and failures, CRM's reputation is showing the scars. Technology is supposed to be the movie theatre, however, and not the movie itself. CRM emerged in the 1990s at a time when consumers in general were becoming better-informed, more discriminating and less brand loyal. Retail banks and insurers were among the first to recognize the benefits of managing their large customer bases more effectively.

They had learned that it costs far more to recruit a new customer than it does to keep and expand their 'share of wallet' of an existing one. But some customers are worth more to a business than others, in line with the

1924	early 1950s	1990s
Market segmentation	Channel management	Customer relationship management

80:20 principle (see page 68), which suggests that 20% of clients generate 80% of the profits. The question is: how are we going to find out which ones they are?

Technology supplied the answer, in the form of 'data warehousing' and 'data mining'. Data warehousing is collecting and storing information in such a way that it can be queried and analysed. Data mining is burrowing down into this suitably warehoused information to see what comes out. What comes out can tell a lot about a customer's lifestyle, predilections, buying habits and overall worth to the business. Once they have this information, organizations can tailor their customer relationships and their marketing accordingly, laced with a hefty element of channel management (see page 32).

> **'When CRM is done successfully, it is like a giant jackhammer that knocks down internal walls.'**
> Dick Lee, 2002

Low-value customers can be siphoned off to a low-cost channel such as telesales or the website, while high-value prospects may be dealt with face-to-face. Information on customers and their relationships with different arms of the business are then merged into one account, so that the same file is visible to all parts of the business – to different operational divisions, to accounts, sales or support. That means that whenever the customer contacts the organization, and by whatever channel, everyone is singing from the same song sheet.

Cross-selling This centralized information can also be used to identify cross-selling opportunities. 'She's got a current account and a mortgage with us. Let's try selling her some insurance.' More detailed individual data analysis can reveal other opportunities. If the bank knows that a customer's endowment policy is about to mature, this would be a good time to suggest another investment product – mutual funds, perhaps. Keeping track of the customer's life stages and events that can trigger buying decisions means knowing when, ideally, to market mortgages, a savings plan for college fees or retirement plans. In the future, we are promised 'proactive' CRM systems that will know if and when to offer us a discount to clinch the deal, as we ponder over the website.

Financial services and telecommunications led the way, but others were quick to follow, and CRM became both a buzzword and an industry. The principal opportunity for CRM vendors was to design and sell the systems that link and feed an organization's channels, its website, call centres ('please select . . .'), physical stores, travelling reps. The systems collect data, analyse it, store it and deliver it to wherever it is needed.

The amount of data needed to make CRM do what it should is considerable, which was a problem in its early days. The Internet now allows companies to store information offsite, and Internet technology plays a much larger part in CRM structures. The increased flexibility this brings has led to increased acceptance by employees – previously, acceptance by people in different parts of the organization has often got in the way of successful CRM projects.

Effective CRM is a business-wide strategy. Integration across customer-facing channels is not much use if the rest of the organization is not delivering on its promises. Ordering goods on the net at midnight is wonderful, but not if they take three weeks to arrive.

> **❝CRM includes every aspect of how you conduct business, from back office to front office to "e"-everything.❞**
> **Linda Hershey, 2003**
> (LGH Consulting)

The future All this technology, by its nature, is expensive and the cost of CRM used to mean that only big companies could indulge in it. More recently, so-called application service providers have entered the market, hosting CRM software which they effectively 'rent' out to smaller companies. This has broadened the market for the CRM concept.

There are plenty of companies who have good things to say about CRM, that it resulted in double-digit revenue growth, improved productivity and increased satisfaction. On-premise CRM continues to have a patchy record, however, with well over half of all projects said to fail or perform below expectations. Its champions say there can be many good reasons for this (see box). One of them is obvious to the customers in touch-tone hell – when the company reached for CRM, the customer was the last thing it actually thought of.

the condensed idea
Bring it all together to keep your best customers

15 Decentralization

As the largest maker of automobiles for as long as most of us can remember, General Motors looms very large in the world of manufacturing, even if its number one ranking today is less than secure. It also looms large in the world of management ideas, having been a touchstone for the concept of the modern corporation for more than half a century. What GM did in the first half of the 20th century still reverberates in management practice, and its most influential corporate innovation was decentralization.

Management has much to thank GM for – it gave them Peter Drucker for a start. Under the leadership of Alfred P. Sloan, GM reinvented both itself and organizational structure, though it was Drucker who analysed what had been done and reflected upon it for the benefit of others in *Concept of the Corporation*. Later, Sloan wrote about it too, in *My Years with General Motors*, famously described by Microsoft's Bill Gates as 'probably the best book to read if you want to read only one book about business'. It has been observed that *Concept of the Corporation* established management as a discipline, but Sloan established it as a profession.

Sloan was a rare creature – a boss who became recognized as a management authority. Sloan joined the four-man GM executive team in 1920, when the company was in serious trouble (he became CEO three years later). Apart from anything else, GM was chaotically organized, having been created out of 25 car makers and a number of component manufacturers. It was also going bust.

First, spending was brought under control, with monthly forecasts and central budgetary control – accounting and finance were never decentralized at GM. Then came the first serious segmentation of the

timeline

1920	1924	1938
Decentralization	Market segmentation	Leadership

> **[Decentralization] increases the morale of the organization by placing each operation in its own foundation, making it feel it is part of the corporation, assuming its own responsibility and contributing its share to the final result.**
>
> **Alfred P. Sloane, 1963**

automobile market, with each of five GM brands aimed at a different slice of the market. Finally, each of the brands, along with three components operations, was made into a separate division, giving them a degree of autonomy over their operations. 'Structure follows strategy', as they teach in business school, and this was, literally, the textbook example.

After multifunctionalism At much the same time, though for different reasons (growth and increasing complexity), DuPont had also divisionalized and decentralized. The prevailing big-company structure at the time was what business historian Alfred Chandler called 'multifunctionalism'. These were hierarchical structures with management responsibilities specialized by function. They had been developed in the mid-19th century by US railroad companies to cope with their kaleidoscopic spread of functions – passenger management, goods management, rolling stock, the rail network itself. 'Line' management was, of course, invented on the railroads.

Divisionalization and decentralization pushed both responsibility and decision-making closer to the coal face, to the people who really knew what was going on. It motivated managers and eliminated much of the time-consuming back-and-forth between operations and head office and, more importantly, separated strategy from operations. Corporate executives had no direct operating responsibilities, so couldn't interfere with matters they knew little about. Instead, they made policy, free from the self-serving participation of divisional executives, who were excluded from overall strategy formulation.

1965
Corporate strategy

1968
Adhocracy

Lowering the temperature

If Alfred P. Sloan had had his own way, the history of management literature might have been rather different. He saw little merit in letting Peter Drucker in to sniff around his firm, General Motors. But his colleagues had voted for it, and Sloan was no believer in management by diktat. As a result, each man wrote a book that became a classic.

GM president and chairman Sloan was clearly resourceful and far-sighted when it came to organizing the business, but he was also very receptive and tolerant with people, as surviving correspondence with his temperamental head of research reveals. The research engineer believed passionately in a copper-cooled engine that wouldn't need water, would make engines cheaper and more reliable, and allow GM to compete directly with Ford.

The executive committee handed the project to the divisions, where it quickly ran into the sand and eventually failed its field tests. The engineer was furious. Sloan wrote him a very mollifying letter, which he got the entire executive committee to sign. The engineer was not mollified and threatened to resign. Sloan wrote again, explaining that there was a lack of confidence in the car, but adding: 'What we have to do is make our people see the thing as you see it and with that accomplished then there will be nothing more to the problem.' The engine stayed on the bench, but the exchange reveals a consideration and tact that comes as a pleasant surprise.

The most important corporate function, Sloan believed, was the allocation of resources. The new structure allowed return on investment to be measured division by division. And that, in Sloan's words, enabled GM 'to direct the placing of additional capital where it will result in the greatest benefit to the corporation as a whole'.

This type of decentralized organization gradually became the norm among large Western companies, who recognized the efficiency benefits of 'multidivisional' or – as it was later known – 'M-form' structure. Following Sloan's lead, divisions in M-form companies have to compete with each other for funds, showing that they deserve them with a combination of past performance and future plans.

Some more than others Today, some companies remain more centralized than others. Japanese organizations are good at empowering factory workers, but less so at corporate decentralizing. Their consensual style of decision-making makes this less of an issue than it might be in the West. Certain oil and mining companies keep their all-important technological expertise at the centre and, with it, many of the decisions.

In spite of a trend towards team-building, many 'decentralized' organizations remain ultimately hierarchical. However, there are voices calling for change. In his 1998 essay, 'Management's new paradigms', Drucker insisted that it was a sound structural principle to have the fewest number of management layers as possible – if only because the first law of information theory tells us that 'every relay doubles the noise and cuts the message in half'. He maintained that there was no one right way to organize a business, however, noting that we had 'come to tout the team as the one right organization for pretty much everything'. He thought that team members suffered from split loyalties – to the team and to their own specialty function chief. But, he said, there has to be one boss because, in a crisis, someone has to give the orders and be obeyed. People have to learn to work in a team for one task and in a command-and-control structure for another. Drucker was always drawn to the middle way.

> **The ability to move flexibly back and forth between centralized and decentralized thinking as the situation demands – that is what it takes to be an effective manager today.**
> **Tom Malone,** 2004

MIT Sloan School of Management's Tom Malone notes that business continues to decentralize, but by a different route. Working from home or telecommuting is growing on the back of new-generation IT. These new low-cost communications give many people in big organizations enough information to make sound decisions on their own, instead of taking orders from someone who supposedly knows more than they do. And when people make their own decisions, they are more motivated, creative and flexible.

the condensed idea
Separating strategy from tactics

16 Diversification

Web overlords Amazon and Google have grown so fast that they arrived at the 'what next?' moment rather more quickly than most companies. Speed is uncommonly integral to the industry they inhabit but when it comes to sustaining growth, they have the same strategic options as anyone else: expand or diversify, build or buy. Amazon, the retailer, now wants to sell online storage and computing power. Google, the search engine, is squaring up to Microsoft with its own office software package. Can they pull it off? Diversification, the route both are now taking, is never the safe option.

Diversification is a classic growth strategy, and every successful company will consider it, at the very least, at some point in its evolution. In its pure form – new product, new market – it is the riskiest of the four growth options in Ansoff's product–market matrix (see page 50), advocated and deplored with equal passion. Diversification strategy set off an early US merger wave around 1916, but it had its heyday in the 1960s and early 1970s, the age of the corporate planner. Top managers regarded themselves as professionals who could manage anything and some built empires of completely unrelated businesses as a result. Harold Geneen's ITT was a stark example of the conglomerates that emerged, acquiring a family as dysfunctional as Sheraton Hotels, Avis Rent-a-Car, insurer The Hartford and Continental Baking.

The conglomerate has fallen from grace since then, at least in Europe and the US, and many diversified companies began disposing of unprofitable non-core businesses in the 1980s. Many of the conglomerates were taken over or broken up, or both. The pendulum started to swing back in the

1886	1916
Brand	Diversification

Agency commission

Shareholders (the owners) and the directors and management of the company (the hired hands) do not always want the same things. The not-always-creative tensions between them are summed up in what theorists call the 'agency problem' which, in turn, can have 'agency costs'.

To the lasting irritation of the shareholders, the agent – management – knows a lot more about the business than they do, and sometimes pursues its own agenda, such as chasing growth to the detriment of profits. Growth means a bigger empire, more status and higher pay for the bosses, and promotion prospects all round. To align the management's interest with their own, shareholders pay them well and may grant them a share of future prosperity in the form of stock options – a cost. They can also sack them, though with some difficulty, or sell the shares, exposing the firm to possible takeover and the managers to dismissal.

Shareholders, in league with exchanges and the authorities, squeeze as much information out of companies as they can. The need to report regularly, coupled with everyone's sensitivity to the share price, has created another cost – short-termism (where management acts in ways that boost the short-term stock price while not necessarily being in the company's long-term interest). Bondholders impose yet another cost. In return for lending money to the firm, they impose limits on the firm's activities or performance.

1990s, though it has stopped well short of a return to the ITT model. The taste has been more for strategic restructuring around a common theme, and the acquisition of related businesses that offer some kind of industrial or market synergy.

Stakeholder muscle One reason for the decline of the diversified conglomerate was the 1980s flexing of shareholder muscle. In many cases, stockholders felt that acquisitive diversification was being driven more by

1938
Leadership

1965
Corporate strategy

1983
Globalization

1998
Corporate governance

Diversification is a corporate minefield.
Robert M. Grant, 1995

size and managerial ego than by any desire to increase profitability. Since most mergers do not, in the end, increase profitability, the shareholders had a point. They were able to press it home by ousting the management or selling the stock, so depressing the share price of the company in question and leaving it vulnerable to predators. The corporate bloodshed that followed, culminating in the record-breaking 1988 takeover of RJR Nabisco by a leveraged buyout firm, has been a powerful incentive for managers to behave in a more constrained manner ever since.

Another justification put forward for high-proof diversification was that it spread risk. There is some basis for this – if a firm is in non-correlated industries which tend to be in different phases of the business cycle, its income is likely to be less volatile. But the shareholders have spiked that argument too, insisting that they can diversify their holdings more widely than conglomerates can, thank you, and that they prefer to invest in 'pure plays'.

Less risky In this post-conglomerate age, 'diversification' is often more loosely applied to include the introduction of new products to existing markets and vice versa. Bearing in mind that diversification can be built as well as bought, shareholders see such variations as less risky, as long as they can be convinced that the motives are sound. One of the most common motives is economies of scope, where several products can share the same resources, such as marketing, distribution, research and development, or even brand names. Another is to extend one's core skills into a related segment, as Gillette did when it began making toiletries, or as clothes retailer Marks & Spencer did when it diversified into food.

Some argue that geographical expansion is preferable to industrial diversification. This provides economies of scale (lower unit costs from producing more of the same) and allows the firm to use its marketing resources more effectively. Multinationals are more flexible than domestic companies, because they can move production around to where raw materials prices or labour rates are low or falling. And this kind of geographic spread provides more opportunities for moving profits or tax losses to wherever they will have the best tax advantages. Rule one of diversification is don't even think of it until the original business is on a sound footing. Diversification will suck time, money and concentration away from the main enterprise.

Does the new market offer better prospects for profit than the existing one? If not, you could be better advised to grow your share of the market you're already in. It may be that the existing market is mature or declining and simply doesn't offer any more growth potential. In that case, diversification might be a viable defensive strategy. But what is the cost of entry, and can you afford it? Finally, do you have, or can you establish, a competitive advantage over companies that are already occupying the intended space?

> **‘All good diversification builds on competitive advantage in core businesses.’**
>
> **Tom Malone, 2004**

While failures by far outnumber the successes, there have been some triumphal moves into new markets, often by leveraging an existing corporate brand (see page 28). Virgin makes ITT look like a focused business. It started as a record label, but now embraces an airline, drinks, cable TV, mobile phones, financial services, health clubs and wedding dresses. Canon has made the leap from cameras to office equipment.

There is plenty of opinion on the wisdom or otherwise of Amazon's and Google's diversification strategies. Some say Amazon should move next door into other forms of retailing, instead of crossing the road to computer services. Others believe that, whatever the outcome of Google's software excursions, it has already invoked the 'winner's curse' by winning a costly bidding war for YouTube. Whether these roads lead to green pasture or the wilderness, they will be required reading in business schools some years hence – guaranteed.

the condensed idea
Is it smart to leave home?

17 The 80:20 principle

Businesses, like life, become so much easier to manage with a few basic principles you can rely on. Management theorists spend much time trying to pin them down, to formulate them in such a way that they will work again and again. But once you move away from the factory floor, where the laws of physics and statistics prevail, things become far less predictable. So it is with some relief that managers can turn to the '80:20 principle', knowing that it is almost entirely dependable.

The 80:20 principle says that 20% of causes invariably produce 80% of the results, so 80% of what you achieve is due to 20% of the work you put in – and vice versa. It's that simple, but the implications, are many and various, for management and, so evangelists insist, for living itself.

It began life as the Pareto principle, uncovered by Italian economist and sociologist Vilfredo Pareto in 1897. Studying the patterns of wealth in England, he realised that 20% of the people had 80% of the money. Investigating further, he found the same proportion recurring everywhere else he looked, in different times and in different countries. And that was that. No one else took much notice. Not until after the Second World War, at least, when two American-based researchers – a philologist and an engineer – disinterred Pareto's findings.

The philologist was George K. Zipf, who restated what he called the 'principle of least effort' in 1949. This said that resources arrange

timeline

14th century

Costs of complexity

GM starts Japanese quality revoution

General Motors suffered much at the hands of superior Japanese quality. But could it unknowingly have contributed to it? Quality-meister Joseph M. Juran, who ignited Japan with his Pareto-based quality ideas, visited GM in the late 1930s to exchange ideas with its engineers. To amuse themselves the engineers had rigged up an encryption system. They gave Juran an encrypted message and challenged him to decipher it – which he did. He tells what came next:

They were stunned by the news that the unbreakable had been broken, and for the rest of the visit the agreeable aura of a miracle man followed me about. As a by-product, some hitherto secret doors were opened up to me. It was one of these doors which led me, for the first time, to the work of Vilfredo Pareto. The man who opened that door was Mr. Merle Hale, who presided over the executive salary program of General Motors.

Hale showed me a research study he had conducted by comparing the executive salary pattern prevailing in General Motors with one of the mathematical models which Pareto had once constructed. The fit was surprisingly close. I registered the incident in my memory along with the fact that Pareto had made extensive studies of the unequal distribution of wealth, and had in addition formulated mathematical models to quantify this maldistribution.

More than a decade later, Juran tied all the threads together . . . and went to Japan.

1896	**1897**		**1951**	**1990s**
Loyalty	The 80:20 principle		Total quality management	Customer relationship management

themselves so as to minimize work, so that 20–30% of the resource accounted for 70–80% of the resulting activity. Next up was engineer Joseph M. Juran, who attached Pareto's name to the principle, though he sometimes called it the 'rule of the vital few'. 'When a long list of defects was arranged in the order of frequency, a relative few of the defects accounted for the bulk of the defectiveness', he wrote, and went on to apply this insight to statistical quality control – with seismic effect.

> **Had I been structured along different lines, assuredly I would have called it the Juran principle.**
>
> **Joseph M. Juran**

US industry did not leap at Juran's theories. Lecturing in Japan in 1953, however, he was welcomed with open arms and invited to stay. He did. Separately but in parallel with fellow expatriate W. Edwards Deming, he transformed Japan's shoddy manufacturing standards over time into world-beating quality. One of the great ironies of business history is that Americans, ignored in their own country, should have given Japanese industry the know-how to trounce US manufacturing – and that US industry would be forced to go to Japan to learn what they had spurned.

Predictable It is pointless to discuss the 80:20 principle with mathematicians, who will blind you with ifs and buts. It is not mathematically precise and the principle may manifest itself as 70:30 or even 90:10. The fact remains that there is, as management writer Richard Koch puts it in his very readable *The 80/20 Principle*, 'a predictable imbalance at work in the universe'.

In the crime industry, 20% of the criminals commit 80% of the crime. Accident statistics show that 20% of drivers cause 80% of the smashes. Even in matrimony, 20% of married couples deliver 80% of the divorces (this figure clearly conceals a high rate of multiple marriage-and-divorces).

After Juran had exported his ideas to an expectant Japan, IBM was one of the first US firms to pounce on Pareto, though not to reduce defects. In the early 1960s it realized that some 80% of a computer's time is spent executing some 20% of the operating code. It promptly rewrote the software so that the most-used 20% was quickly accessible and easy to use. Result? IBM computers became faster and more efficient than the competition, at least for most applications. The lesson was not lost on those who came after, such as Apple and Microsoft.

If you can produce 80% of your results from 20% of your efforts, so can a business, which makes it very appealing. Companies very much want to do what the principle implies, to generate the highest possible sales with the least possible effort.

What Koch calls the '80:20 law of competition' suggests that, in any market, over time 80% of it will be supplied by 20% or fewer of the suppliers though, in the real world, that kind of equilibrium is unlikely to persist for long. Someone will come along and disturb the pattern with a new product or a new twist on the old one. But as firms innovate and compete in more market segments, Pareto will manifest itself within the company – 80% of operating profits generated by 20% of segments, by 20% of customers and by 20% of products. What's more, 80% of operating profits will be produced by 20% of the employees.

> **'[The 80:20 principle] can be profitably applied to any industry and any organization, any function within an organization and any job.'**
>
> **Richard Koch, 1997**

One implication is that the company should always be able to raise profits by focusing only on those markets, and only on those customers, where it is already making the biggest profits. Alternatively, or in tandem, it can give more power and resources to that 20% of the firm – people, plants, sales teams or regions – that is producing those 80% of the earnings. At the same time it can starve, eliminate or greatly improve the other 80%.

Koch warns that the 80:20 principle should not be interpreted too rigidly. He points to the book trade as an example. In most bookshops, 20% of the titles – surprise, surprise – make up 80% of the sales. Should they dump the other 80%? No, because buyers who visit proper bookshops want to find a wide range of books, even if they don't buy them. Cut the range and the customers will go elsewhere. Instead, Koch advises, they should pinpoint the 20% of customers who provide 80% of their profits and give them exactly what they want. Pareto still rules.

the condensed idea
Some things are much more important than others

18 Empowerment

The history of modern business practice began with 'scientific management', which wanted the very opposite of empowerment. Until then, each skilled workman had done his job in his own idiosyncratic fashion. Scientific management's Frederick W. Taylor insisted that they drop all that and carry out the task in the 'one best way', which had been measured and timed to perfection. Empowerment just wasn't in it for Taylor, though he did introduce one small vent for self-expression – the suggestion box.

The history of empowerment in the workplace has, in a way, simply been a journey back to the status quo ante. Its history is not lengthy. In 1977, when Rosabeth Moss Kanter wrote *Men and Women of the Corporation*, a study of power and the role of women in a large organization, there still didn't seem to be much of it about. The book was in the vanguard of a movement to give employees some discretion over their work (a reasonable definition of empowerment), to emancipate them from rigid hierarchies, and generally loosen things up. Today many more studies have claimed to show a link between treating subordinates more like grownups, and their developing more initiative, motivation, well-being and 'engagement'.

Engaged employees have a stronger emotional bond to the company. They are more likely to recommend the firm to others, to put in time and effort to help it succeed and to come up with their own innovative ideas and solutions to problems. Kanter tells a revealing story of a fabric company that made complicated woven materials. Yarn breakage during production was a long-standing problem, adding to cost and representing a

timeline

1911		1938
Empowerment		Leadership
Scientific management		

Letters of engagement

If book publishers and manufacturers of shampoo respect the link between packaging and sales, why shouldn't management thinkers? They love to raid the alphabet for alliterative gift wrap, and University of Western Ontario academics Gerard Seijts and Dan Crim have made a recent contribution to the genre. Believing an engaged workforce can create competitive advantage, they have created the ten Cs of employee engagement:

1. **Connect** – leaders must actively show that they value employees. Employee engagement is a direct reflection of how employees feel about their relationship with the boss.

2. **Career** – leaders should provide challenging and meaningful work with opportunities for career advancement. Most people want to do new things in their job.

3. **Clarity** – leaders must communicate a clear vision. People want to know what senior leadership plans for the organization, and the goals that leaders or departmental heads have for the division, unit or team.

4. **Convey** – leaders must clarify their expectations about employees and provide feedback on their functioning.

5. **Congratulate** – exceptional leaders give recognition, and they do so a lot. Employees often say they get immediate feedback when performance is poor, but that recognition for strong performance is much less common.

6. **Contribute** – people want to know that their input matters and that they are contributing to the organization's success in a meaningful way.

7. **Control** – employees value having control over the flow and the pace of their jobs, and leaders are able to create opportunities for employees to exercise this kind of control.

8. **Collaborate** – studies indicate that, when employees work in teams and have the trust and cooperation of their team members, they outperform individuals and teams that lack good relationships.

9. **Credibility** – leaders should strive to maintain a company's reputation and to demonstrate high ethical standards. People want to be proud of their jobs, their performance and their organization.

10. **Confidence** – good leaders help to create confidence in a company by being exemplars of high ethical and performance standards.

1951	1960	1990
Total quality management	Theories X & Y (and Theory Z)	The learning organization

competitive disadvantage. A new executive, who believed in opening the search for ideas and innovation to all employees, held a meeting to discuss the need for change. A veteran worker, who had joined as a young immigrant, tentatively suggested an idea for ending the breakage – and it worked. When asked how long he had had that idea, the worker replied, 'Thirty-two years.

'It's only a job' Working as part of a team, towards a common purpose, can be more motivating too, and Western companies learnt from Japanese structures like Kaizen teams (see page 114). A Gallup study in 1999 demonstrated that engaged employees could bring a broader range of benefits to the company. It said they were more productive, more profitable, more customer-focused. They also had, or caused, fewer accidents and were less likely to head off in search of another job. Some employees flatly don't want to be engaged – 'it's only a job' – and never will be. Critics regard empowerment as a scam that squeezes more work out of employees without actually giving them any meaningful power. However, the balance of opinion is that a more enabling work environment has positive, occasionally spectacular, results.

> ❛**The problem of large size is a common thread connecting many of the dilemmas people face at work.**❜
> **Rosabeth Moss Kanter, 1972**

If it doesn't produce results, chances are it's not empowerment. Managements are inclined to pay lip service to the idea – 'everyone's doing empowerment these days, aren't they?' – without walking the walk. They may not even understand what it means. Merely asking people what they think about something is not the same as enabling them to make decisions about their jobs. And second-guessing the decision you have just empowered someone to make doesn't feel particularly enabling to the decision-maker. Likewise, breathing down their necks doesn't display trust and confidence in their abilities, though under-supervision suggests you aren't really interested, which can be just as demotivating.

A recent study found that perceptions of the importance of one's job and its place in the organization's endeavours had a bigger impact on loyalty and customer service than all other employee factors combined. 'You're not cutting stone; you're building a cathedral,' as one consultant puts it. Employees need clarity as to what exactly is expected of them, along with the necessary resources to deliver it. The ground rules need to be laid out: the boundaries of empowerment, beyond which employees must not stray;

governing policies and principles; any corporate sacred cows. People have to know to whom they are accountable and in what ways, as well as the consequences of success or failure: promotion, bonus, a pat on the back or the sack (for some, a pat on the back is worth more than a bonus). Once these guidelines are laid down, let people decide the best methods and means to do the job, empowerment advocates recommend.

Leadership effect Empowerment is clearly a function of leadership. Powerlessness cascades down the organization. Managers who feel their own power is threatened or diminished will often take it away from others wherever they can. 'The two sides of power (getting it and giving it) are closely connected,' as Kanter observes. Leadership specialist Warren Bennis (see page 109) describes empowerment as 'the collective effect of leadership'. He believes that where there are good leaders, empowerment is evident in different ways. One is that people feel significant – that they make a difference to the success of the organization. It may be a small difference but it has meaning. They also value learning and competence, as a good leader does, in personal development as well as work skills.

> **When we love our work, we need not be managed by hopes of reward or fears of punishment.**
>
> **Warren G. Bennis,** 1993

Bennis believes that empowerment and leadership create a sense of community, even among people who don't especially like each other. He points to Neil Armstrong and his Apollo team, who carried out a highly complex set of interdependent tasks in order to land on the moon, noting: 'Until there were women astronauts, the men referred to this feeling as "brotherhood" . . . I suggest they rename it "family".' He also argues that, where there is empowerment, work becomes more stimulating, more exciting, more fun. People become immersed in their work, doing it not because they have to but because they want to. Bennis says that pulling rather than pushing people towards a goal is important in organizational leadership. 'A "pull" style of influence attracts and energizes people to enrol in an exciting vision of the future. It motivates through identification, rather than through rewards and punishments.'

the condensed idea
Letting people do the job their way

19 Entrepreneurship

Entrepreneurs fizz with ideas. They take chances. They're driven, energetic, nimble and inspiring. Big business is – well, it's big. Its first instinct is to protect itself, so it's careful and conservative. It's slow to respond and quick to squelch daring ideas. How do you ignite the spirit of the entrepreneur inside something like that? It's not easy, but there is an answer: 'corporate entrepreneurship'.

Joseph Schumpeter extolled the virues of entrepreneurs back in 1911. The most compelling reason for large companies to become more entrepreneurial is to spot opportunities in their own markets before anyone else does. The big boys can tell many horror stories about what happens when they don't pay attention. One of the grisliest concerned Johnson & Johnson, which once enjoyed over 90% market share in metal stents (a tube that keeps clogged arteries open). When a competitor got approval for a next-generation device, Johnson & Johnson was a little slow to respond. By the time it had got its act together, its share had shrivelled to 8%. When IBM told some German engineers to stop work on software that links processes in different parts of an organization, they stalked out and started their own business. It's called SAP and has chalked up billions of dollars in sales.

Larger companies are often present in multiple markets, which means they must keep many eyes peeled. Somewhere out there will be a more focused potential competitor who, even now, may be preparing to make your current customer solution obsolete. Companies need to foster their own skills in innovation (see page 96) or sacrifice growth to faster-moving rivals.

Buy a piece of 'em Various forms of entrepreneurship have emerged – one of the most effective ways that companies can act like entrepreneurs, if correctly handled, is 'corporate venturing'. It has been popular in growth industries like high-tech and pharmaceuticals, where brain power is much of the cost of entry and small companies can challenge the majors with new products relatively easily. So if they look too threatening, buy a piece of 'em and walk into the future together. In pure corporate venturing, the company takes a minority stake in a smaller company with promising know-how, though variations can include non-equity alliances.

The shrewder corporations invest in partnership with a venture capital firm, not least because the latter are ruthlessly good at knowing when to pull the plug. Since half or more of these investments may prove failures, this is a particularly useful and money-saving skill. Semiconductor manufacturer Intel. Since 1991 it has invested over $4 billion in some 1,000 companies, of which 310 have since been sold or been listed on a stock exchange. Nokia too is an active corporate venturer, along similar lines. BT began with its own corporate incubator, but has since learnt its lesson and sold a majority stake to venture capitalists.

Then there is 'intrapreneurship', a term popularized by Gifford Pinchot in his 1985 book *Intrapreneuring*. He defined it as 'behaving like an entrepreneur when you're employed at a large corporation for the benefit of the corporation as a whole'. In most organizations, people are thought to be either dreamers or doers. According to Pinchot, intrapreneurs are 'dreamers who do'. These are the ones who press on with a good idea, in spite of the discouragement or even the veto of management. Pinchot counsels subversion from intrapreneurs themselves – 'it is easier to ask for forgiveness than for permission' – and encouragement from the company, which should allow them time and resources. Unbelievers say corporate-sponsored intrapreneurship is a flashy substitute for what management should be doing anyway at a strategic level.

❛Intrapreneurs are often in trouble because they act when they are supposed to wait.❜
Gifford Pinchot, 1987

1911
Entrepreneurship

1920
Decentralization

Bringing the market inside

A few years ago, Hewlett-Packard set up a trading platform, gave a few dozen product and finance managers $50 each in a trading account and asked them to bet on what they thought computer sales would be at the end of the month. If they thought it would be, oh, between $190 million and $195 million, they could buy a security for that forecast, rather like a futures contract. If they changed their minds later they could sell that one and buy another. When trading stopped, the highest-priced sales forecast was obviously the one that the 'market' thought most likely. And when the real figures were known, the official forecast was 13% out, but the market was only 6% off. In later trials, the market beat the forecast 75% of the time. The 'traders' kept any profits, plus an extra dollar for every share in the right sales range. Parts of the business have since integrated the market into their regular forecasting process.

While pharmaceutical company Eli Lilly produced many drugs, a high proportion failed. Hoping to narrow its chances on picking the likely winners, it involved about 50 employees in a market auction, similar to the one at Hewlett-Packard. By buying and selling the 'stock' of the candidate drugs, they correctly predicted the three most successful. Some employees admitted that their trading behaviour – selling a particular drug they had little faith in – allowed them to 'say', and agree on, what they would never have admitted in real conversation.

A third approach is 'bringing the market inside' – introducing buying-and-selling mechanisms into the company to make transactions, information sharing and even forecasting more efficient. This was very much the style of the collapsed Enron, which is a bad advertisement, but it was Enron at fault and not the concept. Companies have been operating forms of internal markets for years, with one department 'selling' competitively to another, but this takes the idea up a notch. When BP, for example, wanted to reduce greenhouse-gas emissions, it gave each business unit the right to generate one tonne of carbon dioxide emissions. It also laid on an electronic trading system for them to trade those rights among each other. If unit A reduced emissions to half a tonne, it could sell the rights to its other half tonne to unit B, which was still pumping out 1.5 tonnes. No one wanted to be unit B, giving money to unit A, and the company hit its reductions target a full nine years ahead of schedule. Other intriguing internal markets have been aimed at forecasting sales more accurately, and funding and staffing projects (see box).

If BP has been dabbling in the markets, it has also used the fourth and final technique, 'entrepreneurial transformation'. This involves remodelling the entire organization and culture to allow people, particularly business heads, to feel more like entrepreneurs – and so behave more like entrepreneurs.

Agreeing a contract Julian Birkinshaw, a strategic and international management specialist at the London Business School, has studied BP's transformation and says that at its heart is a management philosophy that puts the responsibility for delivering results 'deep down in the organization'. 'Contracts' (see page 129) are set up between top management and the business unit heads, who are then free to deliver as they see fit, within certain constraints. The constraints are laid down by the centre, which also provides various forms of support. The result is a management model with four components:

1. Direction – company strategy, company goals, the markets in which it competes, and its positioning in those markets. This includes BP's commitment to 'be a force for good'.
2. Space – identifies just how much freedom business heads have to deliver on their 'contracts'. They are free from constant interruption and close supervision and given the time to experiment and refine their ideas.
3. Boundaries – the legal, regulatory and moral limits within which the company operates. They may be spelt out in documents and codes, or implicitly understood.
4. Support – information systems, knowledge sharing programmes, training and development, work/life balance services, all provided by the company to help business heads do their job.

> **'Every company needs to embrace entrepreneurship, while understanding that, if taken too far, it has the ability to undermine its own power.'**
> **Julian Birkinshaw, 2003**

the condensed idea
How big business can think like a startup

20 Experience curve

The experience curve says that the more you do something, the less it costs to do it. And that has important implications if you have chosen to build your market share by having lower costs than your competitors – a cost advantage strategy.

Experience curve theory is not the same as economies of scale, though scale can contribute to it. Its true ancestor is the learning curve. T.P. Wright, who studied the US aircraft industry, first devised the theory of the learning curve in the 1930s. He observed that every time cumulative aircraft production doubled – that's the total number made over time – the man-hours required to make each one fell by a constant percentage (10–15% according to his study).

That percentage may change from industry to industry, ranging up to around 30%, but in most it remains fairly constant. Let's say it's 10%. If, after making 1,000 units of a particular product, each unit takes one hour to produce, when cumulative volumes reach 2,000, it should take only 54 minutes. At 4,000 that will have fallen to 48.6 minutes, at 8,000 to 43.7 minutes, and so on.

The theory makes sense, especially if you consider that Wright was studying a labour-intensive production line. As volumes build over time, workers become more confident and quick with their hands. They spend less time scratching their heads or making errors, and they learn quicker ways of doing things. The same applies, in its own way, to their managers.

timeline

1964
The four Ps of marketing

1966
Experience curve

BRUCE HENDERSON 1915–92

A Bible salesman before he became a mechanical engineer, you could say that Bruce Henderson was almost ideally qualified to become a management consultant. History doesn't record how successful he was with the bibles – his father owned the publishing company – but he became one of the most original consultants of all time.

Henderson abandoned a course at Harvard Business School three months before graduating to take up a job at Westinghouse Corporation. There he became one of the youngest vice-presidents in the company's history, earning a mention in *Time* magazine. In 1963, the Boston Safe Deposit & Trust Company asked him to set up a consulting arm for the bank. The result was the Boston Consulting Group – first month's billings, $500.

By 1966, BCG had 18 consultants and an office in Tokyo – a first for a Western consulting firm. That was the year they formulated the experience curve theory. The following year, Henderson's first article in the *Harvard Business Review* put forward a game-theory view of business strategy. It would be another 30 years before game theory really caught on in business analysis. The Boston Matrix, surely one of that city's most famous products, was developed in 1968.

Henderson retired in 1985 and died in 1992.

> **'Few people have had as much impact on international business in the second half of the twentieth century.'**
> **Financial Times, 1992**

1968	1980
Boston matrix	The five forces of competition

> **'The experience curve effect can be observed and measured in any business, any industry, any cost element, anywhere.'**
> **Bruce Henderson,** 1973

Labour costs money, so the learning curve reduces costs over time. The experience curve is based on the same principle – it says that there is a relationship between experience and efficiency – but takes a broader view. Like the Boston matrix (see page 20), it was developed by Bruce Henderson and his colleagues at the Boston Consulting Group (BCG) in 1966. Consultants at the BCG were aware of the effects of the learning curve. During an assignment for a semiconductor manufacturer, however, they observed that a cumulative doubling of production reduced production costs by 20–30%. This phenomenon became particularly visible in the electronics industry as rapid volume growth in those same semiconductors, and hence electronic calculators, personal computers and other electronic appliances, resulted in dramatically falling costs and prices.

Suppliers too Henderson wrote later that, while the effect was beyond question, understanding of its causes was still 'imperfect'. The learning curve is clearly a contributor, as workers become more dextrous. Standardization and automation contribute to increased efficiencies and, as production increases, equipment becomes better utilized. That too has the effect of lowering unit costs. Other efficiencies may come from tweaking the product design and the mix of inputs. Suppliers will also benefit from the experience curve, which should lower the cost of components.

BCG used its discovery in two ways. The first was as a sensor to identify cost reduction opportunities. If a company had not cut production costs in line with the experience curve, it was time they started to look for ways to do so. The other important application of the experience curve lay in its implications for competitive strategy.

To have lower costs than your rivals is a powerful competitive advantage. The effects of the experience curve make it even more important for a

> **It is a known fact that costs are more certain to decline if it is generally expected that they should and will.**
>
> **Bruce Henderson, 1974**

company to grow its market share since, all else being equal, the biggest share will translate into the lowest costs. That cost advantage can then be enjoyed as greater profitability, or used to put downwards pressure on prices and maintain market dominance.

BCG argued strongly that it was short-sighted to allow the price curve to be flatter than the cost curve – to settle for bigger profit margins, in other words. The risk is that competitors will then use price to win market share and increase their own experience curve benefits. If they choose not to, but settle for comfortable margins themselves, these very margins will eventually attract new players into the industry, and they will cut prices. So the market leader should always reduce prices by at least as much as it has reduced costs. That will either scare off competition or keep it unprofitable, and consolidate both market dominance and low costs. These ideas played an important part in the development of the Boston matrix, BCG's famous asset allocation tool.

> **Such cost declines do not occur automatically. They require management.**
>
> **Bruce Henderson, 1974**

Technology and innovation have a habit of interrupting the curve, however. The introduction of new products or processes puts an end to the old curve and starts a new one. Of course, if every player in the industry is aware of the experience curve, the knowledge becomes less useful. If all firms pursue a strategy based upon it, they will all end up with low prices, too much capacity and no increase in share.

the condensed idea
Experience cuts costs

21 The five forces of competition

The four Ps, the seven Ss – management thought is often packaged in this mnemonic, slightly gaudy way. There's a whiff of Barnum & Bailey, cheap gimmickry designed to catch the crowd's attention. Today's most successful management thinkers are certainly in the entertainment business, complete with public appearances, book signings and, if they touch the right button, large cheques.

Don't get the wrong idea about the five forces, however. The phrase and the ideas it represents come from the most serious, rigorous management thinker of them all, and one who is not tempted by the spirit of vaudeville – Michael Porter. The five forces play a central part in Porter's theories of sustainable competitive advantage. He stakes out his ground by saying there can be only three generic strategies for competitive advantage (see box).

You make something more cheaply than anyone else and become the lowest cost producer. Or you make something special that allows you to charge more for it than anyone else. Or you dominate a niche market that others find hard to enter. In deciding which strategy to adopt, managers need to consider in which type of market their industry sits – is it fragmented or emerging, mature or declining, or global? Then, to decide how attractive it is, they should analyse the chosen market in terms of the following five forces of competition. His point is that direct competition is only part of the competitive landscape. Only one of his five forces – rivalry – is internal to the industry, while the other four come from outside.

timeline

1450	1924
Innovation	Market segmentation

Competitive rivalry between existing players What is it like out there? The more intense the competition, the higher the pressure on prices and margins for everyone. Competition will be higher if:
• a large number of companies is competing, particularly if they are all of a similar size;
• slow market growth forces firms to fight for market share (in fast-growing markets, revenues rise even while share is stable);
• there is little differentiation between competing products, and so competition is focused on price;
• barriers to exit are high because equipment is specialized and expensive (e.g. in shipbuilding).

The bargaining power of suppliers Will your suppliers have you over a barrel? 'Supplies' cover all the inputs required to produce – including labour, raw materials and components. Powerful suppliers will raise their prices to capture some of the producer's profits. Supplier bargaining power is likely to be high if:
• the market is dominated by a few large suppliers;
• there is a significant cost involved in switching suppliers;
• there are no substitutes for the input;
• their customers are fragmented and weak;
• there is a threat of consolidation (forward integration) among suppliers, which would lead to higher prices.

The opposite of any of these would put suppliers in a weaker position.

The bargaining power of customers Will your customers have you over a barrel? Customers in a powerful bargaining position can force down prices and margins. The extreme example is a monopsony, a market with one buyer and many suppliers, in which the buyer dictates the price. Customer bargaining power is likely to be high if:
• there are a few, large buyers;
• they have many small suppliers;
• their suppliers have high fixed costs;

1965	**1966**		**1980**	**1985**
Corporate strategy	Experience curve		The five forces of competition	Value chain

Sustainable competitive advantage

If a company makes above-average profits for its industry, it has a competitive advantage over its rivals, according to Michael Porter. He says there are really only two fundamental strategies with which to achieve it and to sustain it.

By pursuing a **cost leadership** strategy, the company delivers the same level of quality as its competitors but at a lower cost. It may do this via more efficient processes, cheaper raw materials or reconfiguring its value chain to lower costs. It can then choose to sell at average prices and earn a superior profit, or pass on the cost savings to sell at lower-than-average prices and gain market share. In a price war, it can maintain some profitability while rivals suffer losses.

With a **differentiation** strategy, the company offers a product or service with unique qualities that customers want and are prepared to pay extra for. It may be a patented product, perhaps recognized as having superior technology or quality in its class.

Porter lists a third strategy, which is really a refinement of the first two – a **focus** strategy. Here, instead of a broad, industry-wide target market, the firm targets a narrow market segment, and tries to achieve cost advantage or differentiation. Given lower volumes in a narrower market, and therefore less bargaining power with suppliers, focus cost advantage is harder to pull off than focus differentiation.

Porter advises firms not to try using more than one of these strategies, for fear of sending out mixed messages. Companies that have used multiple strategies successfully have usually created separate business units for each strategy.

- the product can be replaced by substitutes;
- switching suppliers is simple and inexpensive;
- they are price-sensitive (perhaps they have low margins themselves);
- customers can threaten to take over the supplier or its competitor (backward integration).

Again, the reverse of these positions would make customers weaker.

Threat of new entrants Any profitable market will attract new players, who will almost certainly make it less profitable, unless there are barriers to entry. The easier the entry, the more competitive the industry. New entrants are more likely to be deterred if:

- patents and proprietary knowledge restrict entry;
- economies of scale dictate substantial minimum volumes in order to be profitable;
- the industry has high investment and/or fixed costs;
- existing players have cost advantages thanks to their experience curve;
- important resources (people included) are scarce;
- existing players control raw materials access or distribution channels;
- government-created barriers, as in utility monopolies or cable TV franchises;
- high switching costs for customers.

Widely available technology, weak brands, easy access to distribution channels and low economies of scale will all attract newcomers and intensify competition.

> **'Competition is subtle, and managers are prone to simplify.'**
> **Michael Porter, 2001**

Threat of substitutes Substitutes are products from other industries, and their availability limits a company's ability to raise prices. So makers of aluminium soft drink cans are constrained by the availability of glass and plastic bottles. Disposable nappy (or diaper) producers must remember that, at a certain price, reusable washable versions become a substitute. Factors that may raise or lower the threat of substitutes include:
- relative price performance of substitutes;
- brand loyalty;
- switching costs.

In 1980, Porter wrote his first book on competitive advantage, *Competitive Strategy: Techniques for Analyzing Industries and Competitors*. It included his five forces and was an instant and widespread success. So was the second, *The Competitive Advantage: Creating and Sustaining Superior Performance*, five years later. Some have noted the irony of so many competitors all using Porter's model to differentiate themselves from each other though, to be fair, he offers it as a stimulus to thought rather than as a blueprint.

the condensed idea
Analysing competition – the manual

22 The four Ps of marketing

As the arm of the business responsible for getting the customer's attention, marketing has generated more than a few tankerloads of snake oil. The four Ps, however, has the virtue of being a simple and sound management idea, still much-used more than 40 years after it was first formulated.

The idea of the four Ps is rooted in 'the marketing concept'. While marketing is self-evidently not the same as production, nor is it the same as sales. Nearly two and a half centuries ago, Adam Smith observed in *The Wealth of Nations* that the whole mercantile system had been contrived to serve the needs of producers rather than those of consumers. He had put his finger on the basic idea of marketing – or, in his day, the lack of it. From that time, and before, until the early 20th century, business revolved around production. The 'production concept' meant that producers concentrated on goods that they could make most efficiently, at a cost that would create a market for them. The questions they would ask themselves were: can we make it, and can we make enough of it?

> **'Business has only two functions – marketing and innovation.'**
> **Milan Kundera**

As the age of mass production got under way after the First World War, the nature of those questions changed. People had the bare necessities, by and large, and competition was increasing. Enter the 'sales concept', in which producers asked: can we sell it, and can we charge a decent price for it? The question of whether or not the customer needed it did not arise.

timeline

1950	early 1950s
Supply chain management	Channel management

Marketing, if there was such a thing, came into play only after the goods had been produced, and was restricted to more inventive forms of 'selling'.

It was only after the Second World War that marketing in today's sense of the word began to evolve. Customers had more money and were becoming increasingly selective. The questions that producers were now forced to ask themselves were: what does the customer want, and can we produce it before he or she stops wanting it? That was the birth of the marketing concept, which demands the consideration of customer needs before a product is developed. It also means aligning all the resources and functions of the company to focus on those needs, since it is only by satisfying them over the long term that the company will make profits. The four Ps emerged as a conceptual tool to assist in this process. It was a refinement of the 'marketing mix', a term coined by Neil H. Borden in his 1964 article 'The concept of the marketing mix'. He listed more than a dozen ingredients, to be mixed in varying quantities – a little more of one, less of the other – depending on circumstances. The ingredients were later grouped into four categories by Notre Dame marketing professor E. Jerome McCarthy. These were the four Ps of marketing.

> **Marketing is merely a civilized form of warfare in which most battles are won with words, ideas, and disciplined thinking.**
> **Albert W. Emery**
> (advertising executive)

Product The first element in the marketing mix is the product – which could be goods, services, a destination or even an idea, as in 'don't drink and drive'. Decisions to be made here will include what it looks like, what it is called, its quality, packaging and the level of after-sales support.

Price The second element is price – how much are consumers willing to pay? This is the only element in the marketing mix that generates revenue. All the others represent costs. What initial pricing strategy will be adopted – skimming (as much as the market will bear, coming down over time) or penetration (low prices to stimulate early sales)? What discounts will be offered? Will there be seasonal adjustments?

1960	1964	1966	2004
What business are you really in?	The four Ps of marketing	Experience curve	Web 2.0

The product lifecycle

Like human beings, products that survive their early days have a lifecycle. They are born, blossom and start to fade away, and different marketing strategies will be used at different phases in the cycle. In reality, many products follow their own idiosyncratic lifecycles, but the classic phases are:

Launch – acceptance is more important than profit, and promotion is needed to build awareness. In a competitive market, low penetration pricing may maximize early sales and accelerate the experience curve. If competition is weak, skimming prices can recover development costs. At this stage, distribution is often selective.

Growth – demand is increasing, so pricing can be maintained. Distribution channels are added and promotion stepped up to reach a wider audience.

Maturity – competition has appeared with similar products, and price wars follow. As sales stabilize, distribution becomes more intensive.

Decline – the market starts to decline, perhaps because of innovation elsewhere or changing tastes. Prices are reduced further and promotion is cut back to reduce costs. Eventually the product is discontinued or sold.

All other things being equal, price is the most important factor influencing potential buyers. It is also one of the most flexible elements in the mix, since it can be changed at short notice, particularly in the form of discounts. Pricing is often a difficult issue for marketing executives, and they don't always get it right, sometimes being too cost-oriented or not adjusting to changes in the market. Whatever pricing strategy is adopted at the launch stage, it is likely to change as the product goes through its lifecycle.

Place This is really about distribution, but that doesn't begin with a 'P'. It encompasses all the activities required to get the product to the customer, ensuring that it's in the right place at the right time to be bought. A key 'place' decision will be the selection of a distribution channel. This could be direct to the customer, using sales reps, mail order, telephone sales and/or the Internet. More indirect channels involve a retailer, or a wholesaler and a retailer, and occasionally even more levels of distributor. Making these choices will require decisions on market coverage, which could be intensive, selective or exclusive. Intensive means distributing via any wholesaler and retailer who wants to stock the product. With selective distribution, the channels are limited to a chosen few. Exclusive distribution is via only one wholesaler or retailer in a given area. Place is also concerned with the physical logistics of distribution, such as order processing, warehousing, use of distribution centres and transportation.

Promotion This is where marketing spills over into selling. Promotion involves communicating all the information necessary to persuade the customer to buy the product. Promotional strategies tend to be categorized as either 'push' or 'pull'. Advertising pulls – it makes customers aware of the product and prompts them to ask for it, but it can be expensive. In a push strategy, the sales force promotes the product to wholesalers and retailers, pushing it through channels to the end user.

Marketing promotion is often classified as being either 'above the line' or 'below the line'. Traditionally, above the line activity is advertising on which commission is paid, such as press, television, radio, cinema and billboards. Below the-line promotion involves no commission – sales catalogues and catalogues, sponsorship, merchandising and exhibitions. Public relations, which seeks to build good relations with an organization's various publics, falls below the line. Sales promotions are short-term incentives to encourage sales.

Promotional trends today are shifting from mass marketing to mass customization and the so-called 'market of one', from 'broadcasting' to 'narrowcasting'. And the Internet is changing communication and shopping habits profoundly. Even in an Internet age, however, the four Ps remain a valid and useful construct.

> **‘The aim of marketing is to know and understand the customer so well the product or service fits him and sells itself.’**
>
> **Peter Drucker**

the condensed idea
The basic recipe for marketing

23 Globalization

All right, so globalization is not, strictly speaking, a management idea. It's a worldwide phenomenon. But such a phenomenon, and so worldwide, that it has forced managers to rethink their markets, their production strategies, their supply chains and their sources of competitive advantage. And if some of them believe that globalization is a one-way street, perhaps they should rethink that too.

Like many of the ideas that management has to wrestle with, globalization is not a new one. International trade was in full swing along the Silk Road by the second century BC, and the years leading up the First World War were the high-point of 'internationalism', a frenzy of cross-border trade and investment. It's only the fact that national economies turned in on themselves between the two world wars that makes the current phase of internationalism feel like a novelty at all. So managers have had to deal with it before, though not, it's true, on quite this scale, at this speed and with this intensity. One new ingredient, the one that has amplified all the above, is technology – a coming together of telecommunications, the computer and the Net which has made the world a smaller, smarter, speedier place. That would have counted for less without a second ingredient – the deregulation, privatization and opening up of markets by governments everywhere.

> **Merchants have no country. The mere spot they stand on does not constitute so strong an attachment as that from which they draw their gains.**
>
> **Thomas Jefferson, 1814**

In 1983, Harvard economist Theodore Levitt (see page 201) recognized that technology was driving the world towards 'a converging commonality', that global markets were emerging for standardized consumer products 'on a previously unimagined scale of magnitude'. He

timeline

1886	1920
Brand	Decentralization

The great levellers

Thomas Friedman, foreign affairs columnist for the New York Times, scored high in 2005 with *The World is Flat: A Brief History of the Twenty-First Century*, an update of an earlier volume on globalization. It's 'flat' because the Web has levelled the competitive playing field. But, he said, there were ten other great levellers too.

1. Fall of the Berlin Wall – 9 November 1989 (tilting the worldwide balance of power toward democracies and free markets).
2. Netscape IPO – 9 August 1995 (sparking massive interest in fibre-optic cables).
3. Workflow software – enabling faster, closer coordination among far-flung employees.
4. Open sourcing – self-organizing communities (such as Linux) launching a collaborative revolution.
5. Outsourcing – migrating business functions to India, saving money and boosting a Third World economy.
6. Offshoring – contract manufacturing elevating China to economic prominence.
7. Supply-chaining – creating a robust network of suppliers, retailers and customers to increase business efficiency.
8. Insourcing – logistics giants taking control of customer supply chains, helping 'mom & pop' shops to go global.
9. In-forming – power searching allowing everyone to use the Internet as a personal 'supply chain' of knowledge.
10. Wireless – enabling pumped-up collaboration (personal and mobile).

called it 'globalization', the growing integration, interdependence and general connectedness of the world. Business and investors have moved fastest to take advantage of, and reinforce, this phenomenon, but it is also social, cultural and political, in varying degrees.

Global fabric In the economic department, mutually reinforcing strands of trade, direct investment and indirect investment are being woven into an increasingly global fabric. International trade keeps growing

1950	1960	1970s	1983	2004
Supply chain management	What business are you really in?	Outsourcing	Globalization	Web 2.0

> **Nearly every industry is being opened up to some form of competition from outside the traditional territory.**
> **Rosabeth Moss Kanter, 1995**

as higher shares of spending, around the world, go on imported goods and services. Developing country share of trade has tripled in the last 20 years, helped by outsourcing from developed countries. Foreign direct investment, where a company from one country establishes a business in another, has multiplied, thanks partly to offshoring by firms in developed nations. Investment funds and individuals won't start businesses in foreign countries but they can invest their money in emerging markets, and have been doing so increasingly, if selectively, in recent years.

Corporate globalization has been gathering steam since the middle of the 20th century, as successful exporters gradually put down roots in their foreign markets, to be closer to them and to save transport costs. Over time, a number of these integrated their operations into truly global companies. The next phase saw Western firms outsourcing manufacturing activities to cheaper labour markets, followed in time by services like call centres and software development.

The main beneficiaries have been India, notably in software, and China, in contract manufacturing. Both economies are growing fast, and the two countries may join the ranks of the economic superpowers within the next 20 years, alongside Brazil and Russia. The Philippines has captured a lot of admin work and contact centres, and Asia in general has the largest share of the outsourcing market. None the less, it is growing in Latin America, central and Eastern Europe, and the Middle East. Some believe that even lower-cost outsourcing destinations like Ghana and Vietnam will become more competitive.

Global outsourcing began with blue collar jobs. But now many more white collar jobs, in areas like research and development or product design, are being done abroad, not to cut costs but because firms can't find people to do the work at home. This may well aggravate one of the downsides of offshore outsourcing, a loss of managerial control when surrendering functions close to the core business.

'Think global – act local' The 'great abroad' is not merely a handy addition to the supply chain, however. It's a market, and the really globalizing companies are those with many international markets.

We used to call them 'multinationals', which didn't always have positive connotations, and nowadays they prefer the universality of being 'global companies'. The successful ones, some think, are those that know when to act locally and when to act globally. HSBC summed this up in a corporate tagline, 'Think global – act local' though, on discovering that consumers found it too one-size-fits-all, it was recycled into 'The world's local bank'. But you can act local in the wrong way, as Gillette found during its early days in China. Assuming that the market wasn't ready for advanced shaving systems, it began making and selling old-style blades. Then it realized it was selling more in imported products than the local version. The Chinese knew about the new stuff and they didn't want the old stuff. It's called communications.

Gillette today exemplifies the globally integrated firm, with centralized research and development, engineering, manufacturing and advertising. It has many plants around the world (fewer than before) but they are run from the centre, and country managers concentrate on local trade marketing. Managers are often transferred around the world, reinforcing what Rosabeth Moss Kanter calls the 'cosmopolitan' nature, the global management culture of the enterprise. Others, like Nestlé, standardize production worldwide while product strategy and marketing is national. A third model has quasi-autonomous country organizations that look for synergies with each other. Companies such as IBM are centring certain activities where they are done best, like procurement in China.

> *The "hot line", which used to connect the Kremlin with the White House, has been replaced by the "help line", which connects everyone in America to call centers in Bangalore.*
>
> **Thomas Friedman, 2005**

There is a widespread feeling that globalization is something that 'we', the developed world, are doing to 'them'. Don't be so sure. By the time you notice your first Indian global company, its next phase will have begun. Globalization spreads in all directions.

the condensed idea
The ever-smaller webbed world

24 Innovation

Innovation is back on the corporate to-do list. When the innovative frenzy of the dot.com years came to its abrupt end, big companies stepped back from the new and refocused on the familiar. Now they are cautiously re-emerging from the bunkers. The IT industry shrieks 'innovation' and depends on it for much of its continued livelihood, but new and public commitments to innovate by large firms like General Electric and Procter & Gamble have encouraged other industries back into the lab.

Innovation comes in waves, nourished by advances in technology. That was true in 1450, when Johannes Gutenberg invented the printing press. The advent of the personal computer set off a similar wave in the 1970s, ushering in the information age. In the 1980s it was software and, in the 1990s, the Internet and all things digital. The digital revolution continues, but today's urge to innovate also looks inward as firms turn to their own competencies in search of the new.

If, as Michael Porter says (see page 84), the only sources of competitive advantage are price and differentiation, then innovation is the most powerful differentiator, though history suggests it doesn't always lead to greater profitability over time. Companies are drawn to it as a way of entering new markets and generating organic growth without having to resort to acquisition.

Innovation is not invention Innovation is not a synonym for invention – an invention has to be taken to market for it actually to innovate. Innovation must change the way people do something. In an essay on creativity, Teresa Amabile and others describe innovation as 'the successful implementation of creative ideas within an organization'.

timeline

1450	1911
Innovation	Empowerment

Creativity, which includes invention, is only the starting point for innovation, a necessary but not sufficient condition for it. As Amabile implies, the business of innovation needs to be managed all the way from the creative inspiration through to a launchable product or service.

Innovation isn't restricted to products and services. It might be internal to the business, in the form of new and more effective organizational structures or processes. It could be a new way of marketing or distribution, like the Tupperware party or online grocery deliveries.

By today's thinking, innovation can also be in the shape of a significant improvement to an offering. Build a better mousetrap, as Ralph Waldo Emerson is supposed to have said, and the world will beat a path to your door. He didn't say build a 'revolutionary' mousetrap. However, some companies get bogged down in so-called incremental innovation at the expense of radical innovation. Wharton marketing professor George Day believes that a lot of 'small i' innovation is more akin to continuous improvement. He says this type of project makes up 85–90% of the average corporate development portfolio, but doesn't make firms notably more competitive or profitable. While successful 'Big I' projects contribute hugely more to profits, they are shrinking as a proportion of development projects.

> **One of the secrets of success for companies that demonstrate high rates of innovation is that they simply try more things.**
>
> **Rosabeth Moss Kanter, 2006**

That's because Big I is difficult and dangerous. Innovativeness is made, not born, but many big companies are simply not very good at managing the process. Certain rules of thumb have emerged through successive innovation phases. Ever since the first Apple computer was developed in a Silicon Valley garage, people have realized the importance of giving creative people space away from the burdens of bureaucracy. (The risk now is that these 'skunk works' teams become too detached from the organization, which then finds it easy to dismiss their ideas.) Big, established businesses have accepted that they too must be innovative. In *Winning through Innovation*, Charles O'Reilly and Michael Tushman introduced the idea of the 'ambidextrous organization', which juggles

1951
Total quality management

1980
The five forces of competition

1990
The learning organization

Innovation as 'creative destruction'

In his *Wealth of Nations*, Adam Smith wrote of the 'invisible hand' that steadies markets, even as capitalists pursue their own interests. Alfred Chandler, the US business historian, wrote of the 'visible hand' of management. But economist Joseph Schumpeter, who has enjoyed a recent revival, described the marketplace in rather more violent terms. And when he described capitalism as a process of 'creative destruction', he was talking about innovation.

As much political scientist as economist, Schumpeter (who lived from 1883 to 1950) is being quoted by all sorts these days. His idea that waves of innovation crash down on established enterprises, washing them away

and leaving new ones in their place, seems particularly appropriate to the digital age. So too does his belief that the spirit of enterprise – *Unternemergeist* – is the defining force in the economy. First, he thought that individual entrepreneurs embodied the *Unternemergeist*, deciding later that it was represented by big, research-intensive companies instead.

Certain US politicians have described the economy of the future as 'Schumpeterian', with creative destruction and innovation leading the way. They tend not to mention how Schumpeter's vision culminates – in a form of corporatist socialism, mechanized innovation and the suffocation of the entrepreneur.

inconsistent structures and cultures so that it can exploit (the old) and explore (the new) at the same time. This picks winners in technologies and markets by staying close to its customers, responding swiftly to market signals and knowing just when to kill a product or project that isn't working out. Later thinking, however, suggests that listening to your customers too intently can inhibit Big I breakthroughs.

Harvard business administration professor Rosabeth Moss Kanter thinks that many would-be innovators simply haven't learnt from their mistakes the last time around, and the time before that. In 'Innovation: the classic traps', a recent essay in the *Harvard Business Review* (which she used to edit), she detects the same lack of courage or knowledge that halted previous innovation waves: 'They declare that they want more innovation but then ask "Who else is doing it?" . . . They claim to seek new ideas but shoot down every one brought to them.' She maintains that, with a few honourable exceptions such as Intel and Reuters, corporate venture capital departments don't often create significant value for the core business.

Too small to count The reasons to innovate may be strategic, or linked to process, structure or skills. A typical shortcoming is that, in looking for the blockbuster, managers reject opportunities that seem too small. Some firms throttle innovation by applying the same standards of planning, budget and assessment as they do to the rest of the business. As Kanter points out, creative teams need different treatment, but that often exposes them to class warfare on the theme of 'they have all the fun and we make all the money'. A common mistake is to put the techies in charge. Galvanizing the creative team and communicating new ideas to management is crucial, but not always something that engineers and IT specialists are good at.

> **Companies that avoid "Big I" initiatives believe that the potential rewards will be received too far in the future at too high a risk.**
> **George Day, 2007**

Creativity takes time, and studies suggest that people need to have been part of a creative or research team for two years to be really productive. How often are people promoted off to another part of the firm before that?

Even with the killer idea, companies may not reap all the benefits they hope for. The extent to which they capture the value of an innovation is known as 'appropriability'. Can they protect the idea? How much lead time do they have before the inevitable imitators crowd into the market? How many specialized resources are needed to mobilize the innovation? For instance, if you invented quick-frozen foods, you had to surrender a lot of the value to suppliers of refrigeration equipment. One of the hard facts of innovation is that the profits are often enjoyed by someone else. The PC was invented by Micro Instrumentation Telemetry Systems – yes, who? Generating innovation is one thing, and exploiting it quite another.

the condensed idea
Bringing new ideas to market

25 Japanese management

When Richard Pascale and Anthony Athos wrote *The Art of Japanese Management*, they observed that America's managerial skills were being challenged on three fronts. The first was managerial practice, where doing more of what they already did well was yielding less. The second was a shift in social values that meant people were expecting different things from organizations and from work. And the third? 'The competition is killing us.'

That was the point. The year was 1981. Japan's gross national product was the third highest in the world and on track to be the highest inside the next 20 years. Japan is a tiny country, very mountainous, 70% uninhabitable, with the remainder the size of Cuba. Yet with almost no natural resources, it was growing and investing at twice the rate of the US. It had overtaken previous international leaders in one industry after another: Germany in cameras, Switzerland (who would have believed it?) in watches, the UK in motorcycles, and the US in consumer electronics, steel and a multitude of other products including the zip. 'Japan', Pascale and Athos were obliged to note, 'is doing more than a little right.'

> *Japanese and American management is 95% the same and differs in all important respects.*
>
> **Takeo Fujisawa**
> (co-founder, Honda Motor Company)

Though far from the only one, the book was an attempt to nail down just what that was. The easiest differences to spot were in manufacturing itself, where Japanese companies had studied the American model, learnt at the knees of American quality gurus (prophets without

Strategy by default

'They' say Honda redefined the US motorcycle industry. If so, it wasn't the product of a devilish plan, but rather of the way Honda reacted to a chain of unexpected events. How very Japanese. Kihachiro Kawashima and two colleagues opened a Honda shop in Los Angeles in 1959 with the loose aim of eventually capturing 10% of the motorcycle import market. But the omens were grim.

The Japanese authorities had granted Honda only one-quarter of the currency export allocation it asked for and insisted that most of it was taken in inventory. On his arrival at the end of summer, Kawashima discovered that the US motorbike selling season traditionally ran from April to August. They had split their limited export allocation equally into stocks of 305cc, 250cc, 125cc and, an afterthought, the 50cc Supercub. The plan was to concentrate on the bigger bikes and a few began to sell. Then came disaster, with reports of oil leaks and clutch problems.

The team hadn't even tried to sell the Supercubs, for fear of harming Honda's image in a macho market, but now they had no choice. The surprise was that sporting goods stores wanted to sell them, and they sold them in extraordinary quantities. The enterprise was saved. Later, its 'You Meet the Nicest People on a Honda' campaign opened an entirely new segment of what had been a leather jacket market. By 1964, nearly one in every two motorbikes sold in the US was a Honda.

honour in their own land), and adapted and improved it until they had developed their own distinct production model. They still leave the rest of the world standing in terms of speed of design and production. Their methods found their way to the West during the 1980s, either whole or in part, as total quality management (see page 184), Six Sigma (see page 156) and lean manufacturing (see page 112). Outside their natural habitat, these have enjoyed variable rates of success and survival. Where they have failed, it has been largely because the package that companies bought

1951	1965	1981	1986
Total quality management	Corporate strategy	Japanese management	Six Sigma

lacked two key items – the style of Japanese management and the Japanese individual's attitude to the organization.

Confrontation, no Small as Japan is, it is stuffed with 127 million people who, over the last two millennia, have had to cultivate an ethos of *wa* – harmony – simply not to tear each other apart. So direct confrontation is not socially acceptable. For historical reasons, Western society relies on different institutions – church, state, the world of work – to satisfy different needs. Japanese history has produced a society that tends to look to the organization to satisfy the whole of its needs. It's well-known that large Japanese firms provide jobs for life, though this is fraying slightly at the edges after the 'lost decade' of economic troubles. Even so, they still spend considerably more than Westerners on company benefits like health and recreation facilities. Managers, who all spend a mandatory year or two on the factory floor, identify with subordinates and feel responsibility for their overall well-being. Workers bring to their jobs not only hands and muscles, but intelligence, attitudes and feelings. They are asked to contribute ideas, analyse problems and recommend solutions, and are trained so that they have the means to do so.

> **The prime qualification of a Japanese leader is his acceptance by the group.**
>
> **Richard Pascale and Anthony Athos, 1981**

Western companies are catching up in this department, but the differences don't stop there. In Europe and the US, the command-and-control management style may have become more touchy–feely but it hasn't actually disappeared in many companies. Tellingly, there is no Japanese equivalent for decision-making, and leadership, they say, is like air – necessary but invisible. Decisions traditionally start in the middle and flow upwards, gathering consensus along the way so that when they reach top management, approval is mostly all that's required. That takes time, but it does mean all are sincerely committed to a particular course of action. No subtle sabotage here.

Implementation reveals other differences. If a Western company decided on an unpalatable course of action, like merging two departments, it would probably start with an announcement – and then the grumbling would begin. A Japanese manager would suggest a small change in workflow, then another and, if there was an announcement, it would merely confirm what had already happened. Gradual change is always preferred to direct assault.

This thinking is reflected in top management's attitude to strategy itself. Although its five-year strategic plan is no longer much in use, Western strategy retains a sense of commitment to a grand design. The Japanese plan ahead and have a vision, but dislike being wedded to a single strategy, lest it blind them to changing circumstance (see box). They prefer *meikiki*, or 'foresight with discernment'.

Learning from America Most shocking of all to Western capitalists is the relative indifference to the bottom line – in Japan, people and the society that the organization represents are more important. Now, an extended economic slump and the clamouring of foreign investors has persuaded some companies to rethink their attitudes. A number of them have speeded up decision-making processes to make themselves more flexible, and begun hiring more part-time and temporary workers, a practice previously unheard of. They have even been cutting costs though, as you would expect, by enlisting the help of the workforce rather than by whittling it down. Japanese critics have urged Japanese companies to learn from America and, instead of books on the Japanese miracle, we now have books on the Silicon Valley miracle. There is nothing much about Californian strategies that the Japanese don't already know, however, and the lessons being offered on 'shareholder value' may be unpalatable.

> **We might be tempted to think that because the Japanese value teamwork and harmony and human relations, they can't play hard ball.**
>
> **Richard Pascale and Anthony Athos,** 1981

Recent economic stagnation has been the fault of Japan's financial practices and structures, not of its industrial management practices. Firms need more flexibility to get the most out of today's runaway markets and they could certainly spruce up their handling of non-Japanese employees as they move further abroad. But in their familiar segments of cars, optics, consumer electronics, machine tools, they remain formidable competitors. When Toyota lifts General Motors' crown as the biggest car maker in the world, as it is about to, it will be a forceful reminder of that fact.

the condensed idea
Value people and let strategy unfold

26 The knowledge economy

As usual, Peter Drucker was on the case before anyone else. In the late 1960s he coined the term 'knowledge economy', predicting that the spread of information would cause major changes in society. What management had to do, he said, was to boost the productivity of 'knowledge work' and the 'knowledge worker'.

Academics and statisticians – who want to measure it – have yet to agree on exactly what the knowledge economy is. Some say it is a group of specific industries, such as high-tech manufacturing, computing and telecommunications. Others argue that knowledge permeates all industries. The Organisation for Economic Cooperation and Development (OECD) takes the middle road with a definition that includes high- and medium-tech manufacturing, knowledge-intensive service industries such as finance, insurance and telecoms, followed by business services, education and health.

The layperson could do worse than the following definition, offered by the Work Foundation, a British NGO: 'The knowledge economy is what you get when you bring together powerful computers and well-educated minds to meet an expanding demand for knowledge-based goods and services.' However you define it, the developed world is clearly turning into one. Economists, taught that labour and capital were the principal factors of production, will tell you that knowledge is replacing labour as a major wealth-creating asset. As an asset, it has the attractive benefit of not

timeline

1450	1911
Innovation	Empowerment

deteriorating in value when it is used. In fact, sharing it can enhance its value.

OECD economies are almost all seeing rising shares of national income produced by knowledge-based industries, alongside a higher proportion of the workforce in knowledge-based jobs and companies using technology to innovate. Depending on your definition, the knowledge economy already accounts for more than half of the economy and employment in many of these countries.

Knowledge has always been an economic force, but its power has been leveraged by information and communication technologies (ICT) that can slice it and dice it, extrapolate it and move it around very quickly. Knowledge-based firms, in the narrow sense, are combining the new ICT with new science and technology to create new products for more affluent, more educated consumers.

> **We . . . see the knowledge economy driven primarily by technological advance and rising domestic prosperity increasing the demand for knowledge-based services.**
>
> **Ian Brinkley, 2006**

Adding value Knowledge – the right kind of knowledge – adds value. It can lead to better decisions, encourage insight and innovation, and raise productivity. In innovation, it can create competitive advantage in various ways – knowledge networking can help to speed up and improve new product development, for example. Sharing best practice around the company can cut costs and raise quality. So in a globalizing and increasingly competitive economy, with fragmented and dispersed know-how, there is a growing need to husband and manage this elusive resource.

Even in businesses that don't see themselves as particularly knowledge-intensive, knowledge is becoming a strategic issue – how to acquire it, develop it, share it and keep it. The result is the relatively new discipline of knowledge management (KM). More companies are appointing chief knowledge officers, particularly in the US, where every government agency has had to appoint a chief information officer (who performs a similar role) since 1996. Knowledge management is careful to distinguish

1968	**1969**		**2004**
Adhocracy	The knowledge economy		Web 2.0

Let's talk tacit

Management consulting depends for much of its impact on catchy jargon. A newcomer to the vocabulary list is 'tacit interactions'. It's McKinsey's term for more complex job activities, ones that require 'tacit knowledge' in the shape of analytic skills, judgement or problem-solving ability.

There are more and more people performing tacit interactions within companies. These are the most talented employees and the most highly paid. But how productive are they? McKinsey notes that efficiency/productivity improvement has all but completed its work in manufacturing and, subsequently, what it calls transaction-based sectors like retail and airlines.

The performance gap between the best and worst manufacturers has narrowed substantially, it says. Likewise the best–worst gap in transaction-intensive industries. But when it comes to tacit-based businesses like publishing, healthcare and software, the gap remains wide, suggesting that more productivity improvements lie in store.

The usual improvement tools of standardization and automation won't work with tacit workers, however. Technology must be used to support collaboration (such as video conferencing and instant messaging), the consultancy believes, and management must foster organizational change, learning and innovation. This could be the biggest opportunity of the modern era, it concludes. Is that the sound of lips being licked?

between knowledge and information, pointing out that not all information is knowledge and not all knowledge is valuable. Some consultants distinguish between 'explicit' and 'tacit' knowledge. Explicit knowledge is found in databases and filing cabinets – it can be captured, documented and stored away. Tacit knowledge is inside people's heads, and involves intangibles like experience, judgement and intuition. People are the key to KM – knowledge creation depends on human interaction – and IT-led KM projects tend to fail.

Valuable knowledge resides in different parts of the organization. There's vital knowledge of customers, of processes and products, as well as knowledge in relationships and in organizational memory. There is also the creation of new knowledge. KM uses various methods to create, organize, share and use all of this, including training and the company intranet, alert systems and creativity tools.

There is a steely side to this. If knowledge is inside people's heads, it can walk out of the door and not return – and it does this all the time. Talented employees may be lured away by competitors; older staff retire. In a downsizing world, people are shown the door. So a KM priority is to extract knowledge from those heads and preserve it within the organization somehow. One of KM's tensions is how to encourage knowledge to flow freely while controlling and securing it at the same time. The knowledge economy and its moving parts will be getting more attention from the business improvement industry in future. For much of the second half of the 20th century, the bulk of management's effort to improve focused on manufacturing. Managers and their consultants worked hard and inventively to make things more efficiently. They have been so successful at this that there is not much left to do. All those years of experience and of adopting best practice means that the chances of sustaining competitive advantage through manufacturing efficiency are virtually nil.

> ❛The idea of the knowledge-driven economy is not just a description of high-tech industries. It describes a set of new sources of competitive advantage which can apply to all sectors, all companies and all regions.❜
>
> **Charles Leadbeater, 1999**

More efficiency The next phase was to look for greater efficiencies in services and business processes. This led to techniques like business process reengineering (see page 24) and enterprise resource planning, supported by heavy doses of information technology. Here too the spread of best practice has limited any future potential for competitive advantage. So attention has finally turned to knowledge.

Management consultants McKinsey & Co have drawn a distinction between transformations (making or growing things) and transactions (services, trade, most knowledge work). The firm then subdivides transactions into routine transactions and tacit interactions, which rely heavily on judgement and context (see box). It believes that few companies have yet done much to differentiate themselves by increasing the productivity of those tacit interactions.

the condensed idea
Brains matter more

27 Leadership

There are many intangibles in business, particularly once you leave the production department, but nothing quite as intangible as leadership. What is that follow-me-through-fire magic that leads the way and lights up the troops? Consultants and academics would love to isolate it, distil it and sell it in bottles, but no one has done that just yet. It hasn't stopped them from trying and some believe that leadership is the next big frontier in management studies.

> **Character is the key to leadership.**
> **Warren G. Bennis,**
> **1999**

If there is a market in leadership, its price fluctuates. As the 1990s ended, the most admired CEOs had achieved rock star status and their companies' share prices (and their own pay) soared accordingly. The market soared too – these were the runaway 1990s – but a contemporary ten-year study showed that the stock of companies seen to have great leaders rose 12 times faster that those thought to lack them. Then stock markets fell, followed by the thudding, shameful collapse of Enron and WorldCom, and the trials and convictions of their celebrity bosses. The mood changed. Similarly high-profile (but more honest) chiefs departed companies like Walt Disney, Hewlett-Packard and AIG, and all were replaced by quieter, humbler types. General Electric's Jack Welch, the Mick Jagger of CEOs, retired some time before, leaving a space that investors and the media have yet to fill. Welch, incidentally, said he had only three jobs – finding the right people, allocating resources and spreading ideas quickly. Chester Barnard, writing in 1938, said the leader's job was to manage the organization's values and generate employee commitment.

Whether or not we see a return of the CEO as hero, the value of a directed, motivating leader is not in dispute. As markets and consumers

timeline

500BC	**AD1897**
War and strategy	Mergers and acquisitions

Leading by example

UK consultant Kieran Patel sorts leadership styles into these easily identifiable types:

The missionary – driven by a higher purpose (about the right way to do business, or making the world a better place). This is a leader that preaches and inspires faith, and anyone who joins the company will be expected to convert.

The venture capitalist – looks for the winners in the new environment. Entrepreneurial, on the lookout for innovation, and favouring acquisition-led strategies, a venture capitalist often believes small is beautiful, creating self-contained enterprises within the organization.

The revolutionary – seeks to break the rules, destroy the existing model and change the game. Has a small group of believers who see him or her as the saviour.

The investment banker – dealmaker, operating through acquisition and disposal. These are self-styled managers of a portfolio – of businesses, competencies, relationships, or products and services.

The general – wants to control the game, seeing business as conquering enemy territory through superior strategy and tactics. A general attaches huge importance to detailed planning.

The president – manages the game, as policy-maker and ambassador, remote from the front line. Throngs of advisers both connect and insulate a president from the rest of the company.

change, and as organizations adapt accordingly, the skill set of the good leader will have to change too. Historically, organizations were led along military lines with the leader as general, issuing commands. In today's knowledge economy, what everyone calls 'knowledge workers' are not highly motivated by having orders barked at them. Warren Bennis believes that future competitive advantage will depend on creating the kind of

1911	1916	1938	1960	1990
Empowerment	Diversification	Leadership	What business are you really in?	The learning organization

social architecture that generates intellectual capital: 'And leadership is the key to realizing the full potential of intellectual capital'.

What makes a leader? Bennis, an industrial psychologist, suggests seven attributes essential to leadership: technical competence, conceptual skill, track record, people skills, taste (recognizing talent), judgement and character. You won't find many who lack the first three. But it is mastery of the other, softer skills that may distinguish the great leaders of the future. A leader is not a manager, Bennis insists. 'Managers do things right', he famously wrote. 'Leaders do the right thing.' While he doesn't believe in a single model for leadership, Bennis thinks that leaders must to be able to satisfy their people's expectations in the following:

People want	Leaders provide	To help create
Meaning and direction	Sense of purpose	Goals and objectives
Trust	Authentic relationships	Reliability and consistency
Hope and optimism	Hardiness (confidence that things will work out)	Energy and commitment
Results	Bias towards action, risk, curiosity and courage	Confidence and creativity

'Effective leaders bring passion, perspective and significance to the process of defining organizational purpose', Bennis adds, saying that every effective leader is passionate about what he or she is doing. Perspective is required because people want to know what happens after what happens next. And today's knowledge workers, who can easily get jobs elsewhere, want a sense of significance – they want to know that it all means something.

Going soft 'Authenticity' is one of the newer buzzwords in leadership studies. It boils down to being yourself, if you want people to trust you. If people sense that you are being guarded or secretive – not authentic – they wonder what you are really thinking. It makes them uncomfortable, less likely to give their all. Authenticity says that being open and vulnerable is not a sign of weakness. There has been an upsurge in authenticity training, though learning to be authentic may sound like a contradiction in terms. Leaders who don't eventually get results will lose the confidence of their people. In the world according to Bennis, results-oriented leaders are like ace ice hockey players – they keep taking their shots. He quotes Canadian hockey legend Wayne Gretzky: 'You miss 100% of the shots you don't take.' But they also create a climate that tolerates missed shots.

❛A successful theory of leadership is likely to be team-centric.❜
Owain Franks and Richard Rawlinson, 2006

Like authenticity, 'emotional intelligence' is another hot idea associated with good leadership. Its popularity arose from a 1995 book of the same name by Daniel Goleman, who broke it down into four domains. The first two are personal, the others social: self-awareness; self-management (the ability to control emotions); social awareness (empathy and consideration); and relationship management.

Different styles There have been various taxonomies of leadership styles, some more detailed than others. Montreal-based academic Patricia Pitcher found three types, each with a very different makeup:
• artists – imaginative, inspiring, visionary, entrepreneurial, emotional;
• craftsmen – steady, reasonable, sensible, predictable, trustworthy;
• technocrats – cerebral, detail-oriented, uncompromising, hard-headed.

Each is best-suited to different demands, she said. If you want to build, get yourself an artist; to solidify your position, find a craftsman; and for a nasty job that has to be done, like downsizing, a technocrat will do nicely.

Some are still looking for a dominant theory of leadership to appear. Booz Allen Hamilton consultants Owain Franks and Richard Rawlinson point out that leadership is no better on average than it was in the past, despite clear progress in marketing, production, finance and strategy. The absence of any accepted leadership theory – one with proven predictive value – is, they say, both a symptom and a cause of this failure, but they believe the time is ripe for one to emerge. And if it does? 'This will be the most important development in business management for the next 20 years.'

the condensed idea
Trying to bottle the essence

28 Lean manufacturing

It may trade under a rather prosaic title, but 'lean manufacturing' inspires a zeal that is positively revivalist in its fervour. It is Japanese by birth, and utterly Japanese in nature, managing to be complex, relentlessly demanding and, at the same time, elegantly simple. Doing it is not at all easy, but it does boil down to one imperious principle – 'eliminate waste'.

Lean, as its adherents call it, is about speed and efficiency, though they would say it was far more complicated than that. While it was formulated in the Japanese automobile industry in the 1930s and 1940s, its acknowledged influences go back at least as far as Henry Ford. It was Ford who first integrated the production process, using interchangeable parts, standardized working and a moving production line. Some say he was the first practitioner of lean.

One thing Ford wouldn't do was variety, as it would have slowed down his process. Quite apart from 'any colour you want as long as it's black', there was only one specification throughout, and all Model T chassis were the same until the day the plant closed. Later car makers offered many models, but the price they paid was having to abandon the continuous production line, so increasing throughput times and inventories.

Over at Japan's Toyota Motor Company, Taichii Ohno and his engineering colleague, Shigeo Shingo, thought they could enjoy the twin virtues of

> **'Eliminate the reasons.'**
> **Taiichi Ohno**
> (on being told the reasons why inventory could not be reduced to zero)

product variety and continuous process flow by using Ford's techniques while introducing certain innovations. The result was what eventually became known as the Toyota Production System, which incorporated several new ideas.

Instead of the huge machines being used in Detroit, Ohno and Shingo sized their machines to suit the actual volumes needed. They introduced very quick setups – now called single-minute exchange of dies (SMED) – so that each machine could make very small batches of lots of different parts, to accommodate the model range. And they saw to it that each step in the process kept the previous step informed of its need for materials (using Kanban cards), reducing inventories to the bare minimum. This was just-in-time (JIT) production. At its heart were the principles of low cost, high quality, plenty of variety and fast throughput times to keep up with the fickleness of consumer taste.

> **'Lean production transformed manufacturing. Now it's time to apply lean thinking to the processes of consumption.'**
> **James Womack and Daniel Jones,** 2005

Something different Other Japanese companies adopted some of Toyota's techniques, but it wasn't until the 1970s that the rest of the world, and the US in particular, began to realize that Japanese manufacturers were doing something very different. That was when the Japanese began to make big inroads into the small end of the US automobile market, before expanding into others, such as electronics.

US manufacturers began to visit Japan, to see what was going on, and they returned with the odd catchy idea, like Kanban cards. But they never quite got the full picture until in 1981 Norman Bodek, an American entrepreneur, came across books on the Toyota system by Shingo. He had the books translated, brought Shingo to lecture in the US and started the first lean consultancy. 'Lean' itself didn't enter the vocabulary until 1990, with the publication of *The Machine that Changed the World*, a comparison of the US, European and Japanese auto industries by James Womack,

1950	**1951**	**1986**
Supply chain management	Total quality management	Six Sigma

Lean lingo

Autonomation	Automation with a human touch; semi-automatic processes where operator and machine work together
Balanced production	When all operations produce at the same cycle time
Error-proofing	Designing a cause of failure out of a product or process
Kaizen	Incremental improvement
Kanban	Stocking using containers, cards or signals, responding to real needs and not predictions
Just-in-time	Manufacturing where operations pull required parts at the required time
Mistake-proofing	Any change to an operation that helps the operator reduce or eliminate mistakes
Muda	Waste
One-piece flow	Producing one unit at a time, instead of large lots
Poka-Yoke	Mistake-proofing techniques
Takt time	The pace of production needed to meet customer demand
Value stream mapping	Determining the value added to a product as it goes through a manufacturing process

Daniel Jones and Daniel Roos. Womack, an MIT research scientist at the time, subsequently founded the non-profit Lean Enterprise Institute to spread the word. And the word has spread, to companies like Boeing, Porsche and Tesco. Lean is not touted as a quick fix – the converted describe it as a journey to a destination you never quite reach. And you can't get there on your own because, if you want to be lean, your suppliers must be lean too, because it doesn't work without quality and guaranteed JIT from the supply chain.

Lean starts with a walk around the factory, looking and seeing with a lean eye, to see how the different parts affect each other, on the lookout for waste (*muda*). Waste comes in many forms. Producing more than demanded or before it is needed is waste. So is inventory and anything that doesn't add value to the product. Waiting for machines to process and unnecessary transportation are waste and should be eliminated. Making defective products is sheer waste – don't detect and repair defects, prevent

> **❝Lean principles hold the promise of reducing or eliminating wasted time, money, and energy in health care.❞**
> **James Womack, 2005**

them. If you don't train and empower employees you are wasting their time and skills. If you give customers poor quality with features that don't add value, you are wasting their time and money.

Lean draws on many disciplines, which include JIT, SMED, Kanban, total productivity maintenance, 5S (order and cleanliness) and Kaizen (incremental change). Lean professionals warn against cherry-picking. You can't Kaizen your way to lean, they say. What you have to do is follow the five principles of lean:

1. Specify value – focus relentlessly on the customer when specifying and creating value (not on the shareholder, senior management, political expedience or anything else).

2. Identify the value stream – map how value is added to the product, through all the actions required to produce it.

3. Flow – only after the first two steps can you design processes that flow, uninterrupted.

4. Customer pull – let customers pull the product from you as needed, rather than pushing unwanted products onto them.

5. Pursue perfection – now it will dawn on you, say Womack and Jones, 'that there is no end to the process of reducing effort, time, space, cost and mistakes, while offering a product which is ever more nearly what the customer actually wants. Suddenly perfection, the fifth and final principle, doesn't seem like a crazy idea.'

the condensed idea
Eliminate waste

29 The learning organization

The world is speeding up, as it gets more wired and as people get more demanding – I want exactly what I want, and I want it now. But I might want something different tomorrow. As markets fragment and change accelerates, business has to keep up or die. That's why the continuous improvement that started on the factory floor is now reflected in the notion of continuous change, company wide. The ability to rethink, continually, your purpose and methods is the most important single source of competitive advantage, says Dutch writer and ex-corporate planner Arie de Geus. But individuals can only change through learning, which makes learning the capital of the future.

Hence the evolution of the 'learning organization', which is not entirely the same as one that trains its people well – though it does that too. The organization itself learns and keeps learning, over and above its individuals. MIT lecturer Peter Senge has made much of the running in this sphere. His 1990 work, *The Fifth Discipline: The Art & Practice of the Learning Organization*, describes these as 'organizations where people continually expand their capacity to create the results they truly desire, where new and expansive patterns of thinking are nurtured, where collective aspiration is set free, and where people are continually learning to see the whole together'. Sounds good. How do you do it? With difficulty. Senge itemizes the barriers to creating a learning organization. One is the 'I am my position' syndrome that leads to little sense of

timeline

1911	**1958**
Empowerment	Systems thinking
Entrepreneurship	

responsibility for what happens elsewhere in the firm. 'The enemy is out there' is another – 'out there' and 'in here' are usually part of a single system, Senge observes. A fixation on events, like quarterly earnings or a competitor's new product, can blind us to real threats such as a relative decline in design quality. And while we learn from experience, we may not directly experience the effect our decisions have on other parts of the business. Finally there is the way in which people, particularly managers, communicate with each other, which is usually defensive and reactive, though often in the guise of being proactive. Harvard's Chris Argyris, who coined the term 'organizational learning', has done much work on the way 'invalid' knowledge is passed around as a result (see box).

> **'Learning organizations are possible because, deep down, we are all learners.'**
> **Peter Senge, 1990**

The five disciplines Everyone can learn, but environments and structures like these don't encourage reflection and engagement. Yet if you ask people what it's like to be part of a great team, Senge says, what strikes you is the meaningfulness of the experience. 'Real learning gets to the heart of what it is to be human.' He points to mastery of the five converging 'disciplines' that mark out learning organizations:

1. Systems thinking (see page 172) – a way of seeing the whole, the interrelatedness of things. This means knowing that something you do today, here, can have effects (and maybe bad ones) somewhere else and some time later, and understanding and using the structure.

2. Personal mastery – Senge's phrase for the discipline of personal growth and learning. Grounded in competence and skills, it means living life from a creative, not a reactive, viewpoint. People with personal mastery feel they have never learnt enough, and it's from their quest that the spirit of the learning organization comes.

3. Mental models – deeply held internal images of how the world works or how someone really is. They affect what we do because they affect what we

1980	1990
The five forces of competition	The learning organization

Saying what they want to hear

Lying at the heart of organizational learning is the way colleagues communicate with each other, and for most of them it inhibits their – and their company's – ability to learn. There are two types of company, according to organizational behaviour guru Chris Argyris, who calls them Model I and Model II.

In Model I firms, people only express views or disclose information that company culture (implicitly deploying 'organizational defences') deems appropriate. They avoid confrontation. If you think you'll be penalized, or will embarrass someone, for announcing bad news at a meeting, you keep quiet, edit the truth or lie. So the organization gets 'invalid' knowledge about itself and is unable to detect and correct errors. And for Argyris, detection and correction of errors is what learning is about.

Model II companies deal in valid knowledge, because they have found a way to address issues. Their people are not afraid to express conflicting views and are encouraged to question and evaluate, publicly, what others say. Errors surface and can be dealt with, even at goal or strategy level. Sadly, according to Argyris, there are very few Model IIs about.

see. If you believe Joe is not up to the job, you treat him accordingly. He makes his first mistake and you say: 'See, he's not up to it.' Eventually Joe stops trying, but he's not incompetent, just nervous. For years, a basic assumption (mental model) at General Motors was that cars were status symbols, so style was more important than quality. Mental models are not bad per se but they must be acknowledged and examined.

> **Organizational defences are . . . anti-learning and overprotective.**
>
> **Chris Argyris, 1992**

4. **Building shared vision** – a powerful force rather than an idea, an answer to the question 'what do we want to create?' When people truly share a vision, they become connected, and work becomes part of pursuing a larger purpose. Shared vision is vital because it provides the focus and energy for learning.

5. **Team learning** – aligning and developing the capacity of a team to create the result its members truly desire. Many minds are more intelligent than one mind and teams learn to think 'insightfully' about complex issues.

> **If any one idea about leadership has inspired organizations for thousands of years, it's the capacity to hold a shared picture of the future we seek to create.**
> **Peter Senge, 1990**

They develop a mutual 'operational trust' and, if they are senior teams, pass on their practices to foster other learning teams. Open dialogue and discussion plays an important part in team learning.

Leader needed Senge's 'fifth' discipline, incidentally, is actually systems thinking. He says this is the foundation for all the others and the leader is crucially important in all of this. In fact, Senge says that learning organizations demand a new view of leadership. Traditional leadership assumes that people are powerless, lack personal vision and are unable to master the forces of change. Only leaders can do that – and even then only the great ones. But leaders of learning organizations must design the overarching purpose, vision and core values, design the necessary policies, strategies and systems, and integrate the five disciplines. They must be the stewards – not the owners – of the vision. And they must be teachers, by example, fostering the vision for everyone.

It all adds up to a compelling vision, and 'learning organization' is cropping up on many more mission statements. Do the companies concerned really conform to Senge's prescription? Not many of them. Certainly, team building is widespread and learning organization courses are being run. But to adopt these ideas wholesale is, for most, too giant a leap. Senge may be slightly ahead of his time.

the condensed idea
Learning is the capital of the future

30 The long tail

The Internet changes everything, they used to say in the 1990s. That was just before they discovered that it didn't. But it changes quite a lot of things and one of them – according to the long tail theory – is the ability, over time, to make money out of very small niches.

There was a time when the profitable niche was commonplace, but the age of mass production and mass marketing has crowded it out, most notably in consumer markets. Consolidation has produced powerful retailers. They choose to stock only those items that sell in large numbers, and have reduced the variety of their ranges accordingly. Many small producers have fallen by the wayside in the process.

> **The era of one-size-fits-all is ending, and in its place is something new, a market of multitudes.**
>
> **Chris Anderson, 2006**

This phenomenon has been especially visible in the media and entertainment industries – in book and music publishing and in film production. We live in the world of the bestseller, the blockbuster, the hit. The argument of the long tail is that, in an Internet world, niche products can not only survive but their cumulative sales can equal or even surpass those of the hits.

The man who put the long tail on the map was Chris Anderson, editor-in-chief of *Wired* magazine. In 2004, he fleshed out the idea in an article, subsequently worked up into a book. Both were called *The Long Tail* and both kicked off with a story about how *Touching the Void*, a book on mountain climbing, became a bestseller ten long years after it was first published. The reason was a spiralling wave of recommendations on Amazon.com, prompted by the recent publication of a similar book. This

timeline

1897
The 80:20 principle

early 1950s
Channel management

Anderson's long tail maxims

Expand inventory

Retailers can offer far more variety online than in-store. Some now employ 'virtual warehouses', with products in a partner's warehouse, but displayed for sale on their own site.

Let customers do the work

'Peer production', where large numbers of people contribute to projects for free, has created eBay, Wikipedia, Craigslist and MySpace. User-submitted reviews are trusted. It's not outsourcing, it's 'crowdsourcing'.

One size doesn't fit all

'Microchunking' separates content into component parts – CD albums into tracks, newspapers into individual articles, cookbooks into single recipes. One size fits one; many sizes fit many.

One price doesn't fit all

In markets with abundant variety, variable pricing can help maximize the value of a product and the size of a market.

Share information

Rank by best-selling, by price, by review. Transparency can build trust at no cost.

Trust the market to do your job

In scarce markets you must guess what will sell. In abundant markets, you can put it all out there and see what happens.

1964

The four Ps of marketing

2004

The long tail

Web 2.0

was not merely an attractive feature of online bookselling, Anderson wrote, but 'an example of an entirely new economic model for the media and entertainment industries, one that is just beginning to show its power'.

> **Our vision is to build a place to find and discover anything our customers might want to buy.**
>
> **Jeff Bezos**
> (Amazon founder)

Amazon had carried out two useful functions here. One was that it helped to circulate information about the book and the other, even more important, was that it actually stocked it. For a physical book store, shelf space is at a premium, so the tendency is only to stock sure things. As a virtual book store, Amazon can afford to have a vast warehouse in the middle of nowhere, carrying many more titles than the shop in the high street. Add in digital books (or albums) and the stock capacity soars.

The 98% rule This has a marked effect on the pattern of its sales. A team led by Massachusetts Institute of Technology professor Erik Brynjolfsson looked at the relationship between Amazon sales and Amazon sales ranking, and found that a large proportion of sales came from books that were simply not available in traditional bookshops.

Anderson tells another story, about Ecast, which operates digital touchscreen jukeboxes in bars and clubs across America. What percentage of its 10,000 albums 'sells' a track at least once a quarter? The smart answer is 20%, if you believe in the 80:20 rule (see page 68). The correct answer is 98%. Anderson maintains that this '98 percent rule' applies within a few percentage points to sales by other online merchants including Amazon, music retailer iTunes and Netflix, which rents out movies. In a world of instant access, consumers will look at almost everything. For students of marketing's four Ps (see page 88), this sheds new light on the 'place' proposition.

Plot the number of online sales/downloads against actual titles or products and you end up with a graph that starts high in the top-left corner, falls quickly towards the horizontal axis and tails off to the bottom right.

UNITS SOLD

short head

long tail

TITLES

The extended, flattish element is known as a power-law tail, a Pareto tail (after Pareto's 80:20 rule) or a long tail. The hits, clustered on the left in what Anderson calls the short head, get a lot of downloads in the brief summer of their popularity. The tail, on the other hand, can stretch to hundreds of thousands of products, enjoying lower-frequency downloads year after year – if merchants choose to stock them. It may even, eventually, rival the head in value.

Anderson says there are two big principles to remember when creating a thriving long-tail business:

1. Make everything available
2. Help people find it

> **When you can dramatically lower the costs of connecting supply and demand, it changes not just the numbers, but the entire nature of the market.**
> **Chris Anderson, 2006**

He claims that the benefits of the long tail apply to many industries other than media and entertainment, and he quotes the example of Lego, the Danish toy manufacturer. Traditional toy stores typically stock a few dozen Lego products, with their interlocking plastic bricks. Lego's mail order business, increasingly organized around the Web, stocks nearly 1,000. And only a few of the products on its top-sellers list are available in the stores. Children can design their own products, which are then posted on the website for others to buy.

There is even a long tail of kitchen mixers, courtesy of KitchenAid. Stores usually stock three colours of KitchenAid mixer – black, white and one other colour that is often exclusive to the store. Though it can provide over 50 colours, retailers are conservative in their choice, so that each year only six or seven colours in all are available in the traditional marketplace. But the company now offers all its colours online and, because a long tail appears, they all sell well. In 2005, the top-selling colour was one that is not available in any store – tangerine.

the condensed idea
The return of the niche

31 Loyalty

Management consultants devote many long hours, days and months hunting the snark – hoping for a better management idea, an undiscovered causal link between how businesses do what they do and the size of the bottom line. Frederick F. Reichheld and his colleagues at Bain & Company came up with a winner when they identified close connections between customer retention, growth and profits. They called it 'loyalty' and discovered that, in the best-performing companies, it was intertwined with employee and investor loyalty. Each one reinforced the others.

All those loyalty and rewards cards you don't know where to keep, from shops you can't remember visiting? Blame Reichheld. Loyalty programmes are nothing new, but his 1996 book, *The Loyalty Effect*, made them a competitive must-have as companies scrambled to put his ideas to work and retain their best customers. For those who thought that loyalty had died along with chastity and good manners, Reichheld insisted that it was not only alive and bright-eyed, but was a sure measure of value creation. Those of a certain age will remember Green Stamps, effectively introduced to the US in 1896 and, much later, as Green Shield stamps, to the UK. Depending on how much they spent, shoppers were given stamps to paste into a book and redeem for toasters and glasses. They had faded away by the 1980s, though their inventor, Sperry and Hutchinson, lives on with its Internet-based Greenpoints programme.

American Airlines created the check-in's answer to Green Stamps, and the modern loyalty marketing programme as we know it, when it launched its AAdvantage air miles scheme in 1981. Since then, such schemes have

timeline

1896	**1924**
Loyalty	Market segmentation

multiplied in number and grown more ambitious in the scope of their 'prizes'.

So companies have been thinking up more or less inventive ways of hanging onto their customers for generations, and it was no great revelation to hear that customer retention was a good thing. It was known that long-term customers should be valued, partly because the longer they stay, the lower the amortized cost of acquiring them and the less likely they are to leave. They are more inclined to spread the good word about the company and to buy ancillary products. And because they know the ropes, long-term customers are quicker and cheaper to deal with.

> **❝Once a company understands the ways in which customer, employee and investor loyalty are linked, its management team can use loyalty to shine a new light on its value creation process.❞**
> **Frederick F. Reichheld, 1996**

What Reichheld and his team did, however, was to put the loyalty of customers, employees and investors at the heart of superior performance and to shine a light on the most desirable ones to have. Though they don't appear on the balance sheet, Reichheld argued that these three groups are a firm's most valuable assets. He pointed to the prevailing extent of disloyalty, with typically 10–30% of customers defecting every year, employee turnover of 15–25% and an investor churn rate of over 50%. He asked: 'How can any manager be expected to grow a profitable business when 20–50% of the company's most valuable inventory vanishes without a trace each year?'

Value indicator The fundamental mission of a business was not profit but value creation, with profit as a vital consequence, said Reichheld. Profits alone can be manipulated by firing people. Pay cuts and price increases can boost earnings but have a negative effect on employee and customer loyalty (and the assets they represent). 'Since the only way a business can retain customer and employee loyalty is by delivering superior value, high loyalty is a certain sign of solid value creation.'

1980	**1990s**
The five forces of competition	Customer relationship management

Let me give you my card

Loyalty cards are turning up in the most unlikely places. Maxwell House Coffee awards 'House Points' with each can you purchase. Neutrogena, the hair and skin products maker, is reported to be planning one, and so is America's National Basketball Association.

Designed to reward customer loyalty with discounts or products and services, they can produce satisfying results. American researcher Xavier Drèze, who studies loyalty programmes, tells of a 'baby club' programme that increased sales of baby products by 25% on average over a six-month period. Drèze and fellow academic Joseph C. Nunes have also studied the behaviour of card carriers and have found that the way programmes are structured can make them more profitable.

'Endowed progress', for example, makes customers more persistent in amassing the points required for the reward. Say the task requires eight purchases to complete. Instead, the company sets ten steps, but awards the first two on enrolment. Same task, but customers feel that they have already embarked on an uncompleted task instead of having not yet begun. This increases the likelihood of task completion and decreases completion time, the researchers say.

Some consumers get excited about amassing points even if they have no currency value. Yahoo Answers gives points for correct answers and ranks the results. People none the less devote hours and hours gathering points simply for the pleasure of thrashing others.

The effects of Reichheld's loyalty cascade through the business. Revenues and market share grow as the best customers are kept and acquired, so the firm can afford to be more selective in choosing new customers. Sustainable growth means it can attract the best employees. They get satisfaction from delivering superior value and, as they get to know their long-term customers, can deliver still more value, reinforcing loyalty on both sides.

> **'Loyal employees are sometimes a major source of customer referrals.'**
> Frederick F. Reichheld, 1996

These loyal employees learn on the job how to reduce costs and improve quality, enriching value and raising productivity. The productivity surplus funds better pay, tools and training – more productivity and pay rises, more loyalty. Spiralling productivity and increased efficiency of dealing with loyal customers mean a cost advantage that is hard for competitors to match. Sustainable cost advantage and steady customer growth generate the kind of profits that attract and retain the right kind of investors – the loyal kind.

Loyal investors behave like partners, Reichheld maintains, which doesn't mean they are not demanding. 'They stabilize the system, lower the cost of capital, and ensure that appropriate cash is put back into the business to fund investments that will increase the company's value-creation potential.'

> **'Businesses – especially big businesses – can be very sloppy about deciding which customers to seek out and acquire.'**
> **Frederick F. Reichheld, 1996**

Destructive profit Profit does not hold centre stage in this system, though it is crucial as fuel for improved value creation and an incentive for sustained loyalty all round. The kind of profit generated by this model Reichheld calls 'virtuous'. The be-all-and-end-all profit that has its eye fixed on the quarterly results is 'destructive'. It comes not from value creation and value sharing but from exploiting assets and selling off a business's true balance sheet.

As he says, it's not always easy to tell them apart. The accounts won't tell you, because they look the same in the profit and loss statement. But one way is to measure the three loyalties. If defections are low and getting lower, the profits are virtuous. If not, then the company is probably liquidating its balance sheet and, destroying long-term value.

Not everyone agrees. There is a school of thought that insists that, all else being equal, a growing number of customers will go for the lowest price time and again. Reichheld would, no doubt, call them destructive prophets.

the condensed idea
Keeping is better than seeking

32 Management by objectives

Management by objectives is such a classic principle that many who couldn't care less about business will still recognize the phrase. It was introduced to the language by that most enduring of classic business thinkers, Peter Drucker, in his milestone 1954 work, *The Practice of Management.*

Management by objectives (MBO) is about making sure that you *can* see the wood for the trees. Drucker noticed that managers could get stuck in what he called an 'activity trap', getting so wrapped up in their daily tasks that they overlooked the reasons why they were doing them. MBO calls for a focus, not on activities, but on results. Which is why it's sometimes called management by results.

Drucker tells us that setting objectives is the first of the five essential operations for managers. (The others are to organize, to motivate and communicate, to measure and, finally, to develop people – including themselves.) One of the keys to MBO is that all managers, high and low, should understand the objectives and agree on them. When everyone has their own specific goals, all aligned with each other, and progress towards them is monitored, measured and, if necessary, adapted, the business should be able to achieve the best possible results from necessarily finite resources.

The MBO process begins by reviewing and setting the overarching goals for the organization as a whole. Step one is for the board to sit down and define overall corporate objectives. Then comes the job of deciding which

timeline

1911	1920
Empowerment	Decentralization

particular management tasks are necessary to achieve those objectives, and whose responsibility they should be. Those tasks must in turn be analysed to determine what is necessary for their success, and so on. In this way, subordinate goals and objectives are 'cascaded' down the organization.

Each of the cascading goals then needs to be defined, and a supporting plan of action mapped out. If people are going to be truly committed to the objectives they have agreed to, then they should share in the process of defining them. And since this is management by objectives, not by activities, managers should agree on a 'contract of goals' with their subordinates rather than dictating in detail how the job should be done. As Drucker wrote: 'The manager should be directed and controlled by the objectives of performance rather than by his boss.'

> **In the complex society of organizations in which we live, the organizations – and that means the "professionals" who manage them – must surely take responsibility for the common weal.**
>
> **Peter Drucker,** 1978

So MBO is very much about delegation and was an early expression of empowerment, at least for junior managers. It assumes a certain competence among managers, and to this day describes the relationship between some multinational corporations and their international subsidiaries. Head office accepts that country managers have superior local knowledge and, having agreed outline goals, leaves them to get on with it. Similarly, BP agrees 'contracts' with heads of its business units (see page 79).

Strategy link In this way, the MBO structure is supposed to create a direct link between top-level strategy and its implementation lower down the organization. To keep the whole process on track, progress towards objectives has to be monitored regularly, and the employee's performance evaluated. Evaluation should be accompanied by feedback. For Drucker, feedback means that, whenever you take a key action or decision, you should write down what you expect to happen. Then, as results start to

1954

Management by objectives

PETER DRUCKER 1909–2005

'Think of any management idea that is fashionable today and the chances are that Peter Drucker was writing about it before you were born.' That's how Charles Handy, no mean business thinker himself, once introduced the man they call 'The Father of Management'. He didn't exaggerate. Concepts like decentralization, privatization, knowledge workers and globalization – ideas we now accept as commonplace – flowed first from Drucker's questioning mind.

Drucker was born in Vienna, spent his twenties in Hitler's Germany and worked briefly in London before settling in the US in 1939. Seven years later he published *Concept of the Corporation*, an intimate analysis of General Motors and its management, which irritated its subject by asking questions about the role of business in society. That was typical of Drucker. Mistrustful of both big government and unrestrained market forces, he believed that good management and its example could save the world from itself.

He was critical of the assembly line legacy of Frederick Taylor (see page 152) and felt workers should be treated as resources – brain workers – not costs. He did not advocate too much empowerment, however, nor too much management control, preferring to steer a middle course between anarchy on the one hand and stifled creativity on the other.

Drucker's interests ranged far beyond the world of business – he was fascinated by the behaviour of government and of voluntary organizations. Indeed, of his 35 books, fewer than half were devoted to management. He did not care to be called a 'management guru', once observing that journalists used the word 'guru' only because 'charlatan' was too long for a headline.

become available, you check regularly to see how expectations compare with what actually happens. This feedback can then be used to decide what you are good at, what you are bad at, where you need to change and where you should press on.

The achievers, those who meet their objectives, are then rewarded. In MBO's undiluted form, non-achievers are punished. Drucker's work with General Electric in the 1940s provided much of the basis for MBO – and GE managers who didn't meet their targets at the time were fired.

One weakness of MBO is that all this goal-setting and revising generates lots of paperwork and is very time-consuming. Another is that, since it rests heavily on the objectives themselves, it is important to select goals

> **❝In the knowledge-based organization, all members have to be able to control their work by feedback from their results to their objectives.❞**

Peter Drucker, 1993

that, by their nature, can succeed – smart goals. In the 1980s and 1990s, SMART became a popular acronym for the qualities demanded by MBO objectives. They ought to be:

Specific – vague and generalized won't do.
Measurable – the objective should be quantifiable.
Achievable – not too easy, not impossible.
Realistic – given the resources available.
Time-related – set a deadline.

No competent manager would suggest doing away with objectives but, as a complete theory, classical MBO is not in active use. Given today's increasing acceptance of holistic systems thinking, the MBO concept is seen as too linear, and too dismissive of context and human nature. Nor is it particularly well-suited to a fast-moving information age in which changing assumptions and goals can make yesterday's planning redundant all too quickly.

Results-based management that rewards achievers and directly or indirectly penalizes others can have distorting effects on team-building, morale and even ethical behaviour, as employees 'work the numbers'. As with many other influential management ideas, MBO has sometimes been subjected to overly harsh criticism. Drucker can't have minded much and was at pains himself to downplay his theory's importance. 'It's just another tool', he is reported to have said. 'It is not the great cure for management inefficiency . . . MBO works if you know the objectives. Ninety percent of the time you don't.'

the condensed idea
Results, results, results

33 Market segmentation

There's much blog-talk of the death of the mass market these days. In which case, it has been a long time a-dying. The mass media, cardiograms of the mass market, have been losing viewers and readers since the 1970s – at least in the US, where the mass market was invented. It's true, none the less, that a proliferation of new media has forced the pace of its decline in recent years. And the zoom factor of market segmentation, the opposite of mass marketing, has been closing in on individual consumers with the persistence of a spy satellite.

The mass market was created by American companies like Sears Roebuck, DuPont and General Electric, hand in hand with the march of the railroads and the telegraph. It grew rapidly between the 1880s and the 1920s. Mass marketing, on the other hand, only got into its stride from 1920 onwards with the spread of 'sound-receiving devices' – the radio. Television arrived shortly before the Second World War and by the 1960s an advertiser could reach 80% of American women with a TV commercial aired simultaneously on ABC, CBS and NBC.

Early mass marketing was not subtle, but it was egalitarian. It beamed the same message and sold the same products to everyone. Segmentation, however, says that people are not all the same and have different needs and aspirations. That they also have different wallets was recognized by General Motors' Alfred P. Sloan as early as 1924, when he offered the

timeline

public 'a car for every purse and purpose'. GM was pioneering segmentation, by income.

'Differing preferences' It was not until 1956 that Wendell Smith formalized this idea with an essay, 'Product differentiation and market segmentation as alternative marketing strategies', in the *Journal of Marketing*. He wrote: 'Market segmentation involves viewing a heterogeneous market as a number of smaller homogeneous markets, in response to differing preferences, attributable to the desires of consumers for more precise satisfaction of their varying wants.' Smith was head of market research at RCA, maker of radio and TV sets, so his interest was not entirely academic.

> **[Lifestyle is] the distinctive or characteristic mode of living of a whole society or segment thereof.**
>
> **William Lazer, 1963**

Segmentation has drilled down into many more layers of customer detail since Smith's time, as consumers have evolved from wanting what their neighbours had to wanting to be special. In 1963, William Lazar introduced the concept of 'lifestyles' to marketing, as a system of attitudes and values, opinions and interests – of either a group or an individual. In search of carefully defined and, it's hoped, suitably receptive customers, classic segmentation first divides the total market into consumer and industrial segments. The consumer market is then broken down into more helpful characteristics via four broad prisms: **demographics** – including age, gender, family size and lifecycle, social class, education, income, occupation and religion; **geography** – region, country, urban or rural, and climate; **psychographics** – lifestyle, values, opinions and attitude; and **behaviour** – what benefits do they seek, brand loyalty and who makes the buying decision? Apply those to business customers and you get a comparable list, including location, business type, size, usage rate, who makes the buying decisions and how. Once you have defined a segment, you need to be sure it's worth the time and effort to continue by defining a marketing mix. It should tick the following boxes: sufficiently different,

1924
Market segmentation

1964
The four Ps of marketing

2004
Web 2.0

potentially profitable, accessible and likely to be responsive. Segmentation overkill can be expensive.

So pervasive is the philosophy of segmentation that it is hard to find a company that admits to being in the mass market any more, even among those that once personified it. Procter & Gamble, whose Tide has been America's biggest-selling laundry detergent for more than half a century, claims it has no mass market brands – every one is targeted. McDonald's, likewise, is not a mass marketer, though it admits to being a 'big' marketer. It is more ironic than one could hope for that one of the few companies still calling itself a 'mass market manufacturer' is . . . RCA.

> **The most important characteristic of this new market of "ones" is that we're talking with one another, and we're telling one another the truth about your products. Marketing is much less interesting than these conversations.**
>
> **Adriana Cronin-Lukas, 2003** (blogger)

'Pull' marketing towards you As the focus tightens, 'mass customization' allows customers to choose from a range of variants to a standard product. Not all companies have had happy experiences with this strategy, but Dell has used it to good effect in the personal computer industry. Land's End, the catalogue retailer, now tailors certain individual items of clothing to customer-supplied measurements. 'Micromarketing' sometimes calls itself 'one-to-one' – as opposed to 'one-to-many' – marketing, using email and the Web to connect with individual preferences. The website that announces 'People who bought [what you just bought] also bought . . .' is doing micromarketing. So are RSS Web feeds that allow you to 'pull' marketing towards you, by specifying the diet of information on which you want regularly to be fed. The Web has given niche brands a platform from which to compete on more or less equal terms with mass brands, as they develop cosy relationships with communities of Web users.

'Paid search' is another form of self-selecting marketing, and the fastest-growing form of online advertising. These are the 'sponsored links' or ads that beckon – or not – when you use a search engine. The highest-bidding advertiser sits at the top of the list, where it gets more clicks, and pays the search engine every time someone clicks through to their site – 'pay per click'. Google was forecast to take the biggest single share of UK advertising revenues in 2007, a spectral indicator for mass marketing, not

Formative fifties

Market segmentation was a milestone in the evolution of marketing from the early days of seat-of-the-pants through to the grownup and documented discipline it has become. Many other marketing milestones were, like segmentation, formulated in the 1950s while infant television was transforming advertising. Until then, for most companies the 'market' was simply what you sold to, and you sold as much as you could. But in 1950 Neil Borden introduced the 'marketing mix' concept, holding that successful selling involved ingredients like product planning, pricing, branding and distribution – the antecedents of the 'four Ps' (see page 88).

At much the same time, others were refining thinking on the 'product lifecycle' and on 'brand image'(see page 28). General Electric president John McKitterick pulled these strands together, and introduced the 'marketing concept', in a 1957 speech entitled 'What is the marketing management concept?' His answer was a 'customer-oriented, integrated, profit-oriented' philosophy of business.

Abe Schuhman coined the term 'marketing audit' in 1959, as a systematic examination of every aspect of sales, marketing, customer service, and even relevant operations, to see how well and cost-effectively they are helping the organization to reach its goals. When the 1960s opened with Ted Levitt's 'Marketing myopia' fusillade (see page 200), marketing already had a secure grounding, in theory if not in practice.

to mention UK commercial television. A well-worn ad agency parable is the one about the marketing manager who said he knew he wasted 50% of his advertising budget – he just didn't know which 50%. Wherever he is, he must love digital Internet advertising, which tells him just how effectively his money is being spent, as well as bringing him all that precious information that customers are obligingly tap-tapping into his database. Persuasion is becoming more of a science than the art it used to be.

the condensed idea
From shotgun
to telescopic sight

34 Mergers and acquisitions

The hostile takeover is about as exhilarating as it gets up at head office. It's the chief executive suite as campaign tent, complete with hurrying advisers, councils-of-war and swift-changing tactics. For leaders who favour the military style, this is as close as it gets to being a real general – the plan, the strike, the capitulation and the prize. Sadly for them, the hostile bid is becoming less fashionable, but acquisition remains a perfectly reasonable, if usually less dramatic, strategic option for companies of all kinds.

Mergers and acquisitions – 'M&A' in investment-banker speak – attract more public attention than anything a big company does except, perhaps, firing half the workforce or going bust. Typically, they happen when one company acquires all the assets and liabilities of another. Is there a difference between a merger and an acquisition? Not very often. A true merger is a marriage of equals in which shares are pooled in a new company, and these are unusual. Car makers Daimler-Benz and Chrysler merged in this spirit of equality in 1998, taking a new name – DaimlerChrysler – to reflect this. Even so, American commentators now complain it was a de facto takeover, with German management and know-how calling the shots – and even, it's said, now preparing to sell Chrysler.

Unlike DaimlerChrysler, most 'mergers' are obvious takeovers in which the separate identity of one party disappears, if not immediately, then over

timeline

500 BC	1897
War and strategy	Mergers and acquisitions

time. The M-word is mere diplomacy, a face-saving veil for the acquired. Whatever form they take, mergers are driven by one overriding motive: to make one and one equal three. Some call it 'synergy' or 'adding value', but it boils down to creating a business worth more than the sum of its parts. Quite often though, it ends up as less, as we'll see later.

Up and down, or sideways Classically, there are three kinds of merger. 'Horizontal' mergers mean acquiring a company in the same industry, to grow market share the quick way. 'Vertical' mergers involve vertical integration, by buying a supplier or a distribution channel, and are usually about controlling costs. Finally, in what's known in the US as a 'conglomerate' merger, a firm buys an unrelated business as a form of diversification.

> **It's now time for all of us – those who supported the merger and those who opposed it – to pull together for the benefit of the company.**
>
> **Carly Fiorina,** 1999 (former Hewlett-Packard president, on the company's 'merger' with Compaq)

The synergies that the buyer seeks can be found in various places. The most common is by eliminating duplications to cut costs. Simply closing down one head office can save worthwhile sums of money. Two human resources departments can be collapsed into one and the same goes for accounts and finance, perhaps marketing, and research and development. This has its ugly side, since most of the savings come from sacking people.

Though it applies to most mergers, eliminating duplication is easiest in horizontal takeovers, where the organizations may be mirror images of each other. That's also true of the next synergy, economies of scale – if you are buying more, it'll be cheaper, whether sub-assemblies or paperclips. There are sometimes tax advantages in mergers if, say, the target has tax losses that the acquirer can put to good use.

These are generic benefits from going out and buying a company, but they might be more specific: to acquire new technology, expand into new

1916	1938	1965
Diversification	Leadership	Corporate strategy

Higher power

Mergers usually fail because companies foul up the integration phase, but occasionally they don't even get that far. What was billed as the world's biggest merger was halted in its tracks by the competition authorities of the European Union in 2001.

General Electric had offered $41 billion to acquire Honeywell Internationalin 2000. GE was attracted by Honeywell's aerospace businesses which, together with its industrial system and plastics activities, fitted neatly with its own. Jack Welch, the company's CEO, had even deferred his retirement for a year to see the deal through.

The merger would have increased the size of GE, already one of the world's largest companies, by nearly one-third.

The US Justice Department gave it the green light, insisting only that GE sell off its military helicopter business for security purposes. But the Europeans weren't having it. On competition grounds, and for the first time, they forbade a merger that had earlier been passed by the US authorities. Honeywell had already ceded control on major operational and hiring decisions to GE. 'This shows you are never too old to get surprised', said a disappointed Welch.

product or geographic markets, or even – it has happened – to kidnap a particular CEO. A 'reverse' takeover or merger happens when an unquoted company wants a stock exchange listing but not the trouble and expense of an initial public offering (IPO). It buys a listed firm, disposing of its unwanted assets and reversing itself into the shell, like a hermit crab. WPP, one of the world's largest advertising groups, was shopping trolley manufacturer Wire and Plastic Products until present chairman Martin Sorrell 'reversed' his interests into it in the mid-1980s.

Fewer than half of all mergers work. That's to say that the failures don't add the value envisaged when the deal was done. Sometimes it's because the strategy was misguided in the first place. More often it's because companies make a mess of integrating the acquired business into the existing one. As post-merger integration (PMI) specialists keep saying, it's not over when the deal is done – it has just begun.

A common failing is the inability to knit two different cultures into one. Staff in the acquired company are invariably fearful and mistrustful of their new owners. They need to be reassured and respected, and made to feel part of the new enterprise. Management should concentrate rather more on this issue and less on the new logo. Another pitfall is to reproduce in the new organization practices and process that didn't work very well in the old. Perhaps most important is that the acquirer should have a vision and a plan ready to go on day one – remember the Iraq war – and that everyone in the organization should know what it is. If PMI doesn't work, it can precipitate mass defections of the best staff, customers, suppliers and investors.

> **❝I always said that mega-mergers were for megalomaniacs.❞**
>
> **David Ogilvy** (advertising executive)

Paying too much One preprogrammed reason why some acquisitions don't add value is that management paid too much in the first place. That's inclined to happen in contested auctions for a company, when the CEO cares more about the size of his empire than about doing the sums. Extravagant prices are more likely to be paid when the business world is gripped by yet another fit of merger mania. These come and go, dating back to America's 1897–1904 wave, which ended in a stock market crash and anti-trust legislation. Most of the 1980s and the latter half of the 1990s were years of peak M&A activity in both the US and the UK. The 1980s spawned the corporate raider, the 'mega-merger' and a rise in foreign takeovers. The 1990s wave, which ended when the high-tech stock market bubble burst in 2000, was less about sheer size than about strategic restructuring.

M&A waves are fuelled by high stock prices, which give companies cheap currency in which to pay, and/or cheap debt, which allows them to pay in cash instead of shares. Cheap borrowing has nourished a new breed of acquirer – the private equity fund. Acquisition is the sum of their strategy, which is to buy companies relatively cheaply, squeeze out the fat and sell them on.

the condensed idea
Buy or build? Buy

35 Organizational excellence

Many esoteric works on management never make it past the campus gates. Others can influence the way companies are organized and run, though they usually have to filter their way through the consultancy profession first. A limited number of management books deliver an idea that's gripping enough to be read by senior management itself, drinking directly from the source. But only one has single-handedly created a whole new industry – *In Search of Excellence*, by McKinsey consultants Tom Peters and Robert Waterman.

You could say that the book created two new industries: the mass business book industry and the Tom Peters industry. It appeared like a torch of hope to a benighted corporate America, that felt it had lost its way in the dark. Battered by competition from the most unlikely source, in markets they had dominated proudly only a few years before, American managers reached for Peters and Waterman like a cartoon man-on-knees-in-desert reaches for water. Their message was that there were excellent companies in America, and that excellence was there for the taking, if only managers could concentrate on the customer, realize the power of their people and do it with passion.

This was do-it-yourself management consultancy in the most readable form, and people bought it in their millions. It remains the best-selling business book ever and launched a highly lucrative career for Tom Peters, with his personal appearances, books, videos and TV series.

timeline

1450	1911
Innovation	Entrepreneurship

The seven Ss

Organizations are complicated and, if you're thinking about changing one, it helps to have a framework that directs your attention to the right places. In preparing *In Search of Excellence*, Peters and Waterman developed just such a framework and, after some alliterative pulling and pushing, called it the seven Ss. It identified seven interdependent variables within the organization: structure, strategy, systems, staff, style, skills and shared values

The first three variables (structure, strategy and systems) represented the organization's 'hardware' and the other four its 'software'. Richard Pascale and Anthony Athos, who assisted with the concept, used it as the basis for their *The Art of Japanese Management* (see page 100). This argued that American managers tended to overfocus on the 'hard' bits and that, unlike their Japanese counterparts, they were not awfully good at the 'soft' ones.

Peters and Waterman felt that the seven Ss reminded professional managers that 'soft is hard'. It told them: 'All that stuff you have been dismissing for so long as the intractable, irrational, intuitive, informal organization can be managed . . . Not only are you foolish to ignore it, but here's a way to think about it.'

Published in 1982, *In Search of Excellence* was based on a simple methodology, which was part of its charm. The authors screened a number of companies on the basis of 'measures of long-term superiority', looking at 20-year compound asset and equity growth, ratios of market value to book value, return on capital, return on equity and return on sales. Other criteria were industry rankings and innovativeness. Emerging unscathed at the end of this obstacle course were 43 companies, 14 of which were singled out as having shown up especially well on all counts. They were Boeing, Caterpillar, Dana, Delta Airlines, Digital Equipment, Emerson Electric, Fluor, Hewlett-Packard, IBM, Johnson & Johnson, McDonald's, Procter & Gamble and 3M.

1938	**1960**	**1981**	**1982**	**1990s**
Leadership	Theories X & Y (and Theory Z)	Japanese management	Organizational excellence	Customer relationship management

Right enough to be wrong The authors noted that professionalism in management was often equated with 'hard-headed rationality'. There was a belief that well-trained professional managers could manage anything, that all decisions could be justified by detached analysis. That was just right enough to be dangerously wrong, they maintained, and it had led America astray. 'It doesn't teach us to love the customers', they said. 'It doesn't show how strongly workers can identify with the work they do if we give them a little say-so.' They took a pop at other practices – inspector-generated instead of self-generated quality control, a failure to nourish product champions, a lack of obsession with customer service. Rationality 'doesn't show, as [Harvard business administration professor] Anthony Athos puts it, that "good managers make meanings for people, as well as money" .' Peters and Waterman also took issue with the negative view that most companies took of their people. We want to feel good about ourselves, and the number of us that think we're above average is way above average. Yet companies set impossibly high targets, punish tiny failures and kill the spirit of the champion even as they call for innovation. 'Excellent' companies didn't behave in this way. The two consultants pinpointed eight common attributes that characterized the chosen few:

> **'Service, quality, reliability are strategies aimed at loyalty and long-term revenue stream growth.'**
>
> **Tom Peters and Robert Waterman, 1982**

1. A bias for action – they got on with it. They might have been analytical over decision-making but they were not paralysed by it. In many, standard operating procedure was 'do it, fix it, try it'.

2. Close to the customer – they learnt from the people they served, providing unparalleled quality, service and reliability (virtues that work and last). Many got their best product ideas from listening intently to customers.

3. Autonomy and entrepreneurship – they fostered leaders and innovators and were hives of champions. They didn't hold people on so short a rein that they couldn't be creative, but encouraged risk-taking and supported good tries.

4. Productivity through people – they treated the rank and file as the basic source of quality and productivity gain. No we/they attitudes to labour and no regarding capital investment as the principal source of productivity improvement – they had respect for the individual.

5. Hands-on, value-driven – IBM's Thomas Watson and Hewlett-Packard's William Hewlett were legendary for 'management by walking about'. McDonald's Ray Croc regularly visited outlets and assessed them on the fast food chain's dearly held factors of quality, service, cleanliness and value.

6. Stick to the knitting – Johnson & Johnson's former chairman, Robert Johnson, used to say: 'Never acquire a business you don't know how to run.' Edward Harness, ex-CEO of Procter & Gamble said: 'This company has never left its base. We seek to be anything but a conglomerate.'

7. Simple form, lean staff – none of the excellent companies was organized in a matrix structure (where staff report to both a project manager and a function manager). They had 'elegantly simple' structures and systems, and a lean top-level of staff.

8. Simultaneous loose–tight properties – they were both centralized and decentralized, mostly pushing autonomy down to the shop floor or product development team. Yet, when it came to their few most important core values, they were fanatical centralists.

Sadly, in many cases, the excellence did not endure. Within five years, two-thirds of the companies on the list were in trouble of one kind or another and one had actually gone out of business. It didn't seem to matter. Peters and Waterman had inspired a generation of businesspeople with the thought that something better was possible, and much of their advice is as pertinent now as it was then. While the two have since pursued separate writing careers, Peters achieved the kind of superstar status that allowed him to begin his third book, *Thriving on Chaos*, with the line: 'There are no excellent companies.'

> **There is good news from America. Good management practice is not resident only in Japan.**
> **Tom Peters and Robert Waterman, 1982**

the condensed idea
Eight attributes of excellent companies

36 Outsourcing

In 2003, Procter & Gamble caused a few jaws to drop by outsourcing its IT functions to Hewlett-Packard, its human resources department to IBM and its facilities management to Jones Lang LaSalle. It reasoned that specialists in each process would be able to beef up efficiency and service. Not only has it not been disappointed, but it has been pleasantly surprised at the scale of the improvement. So far, the exercise has been a classic example of why management reaches for outsourcing.

Not all outsourcing fits that description, by any means. Many who have tried it say it is very difficult to pull off, and the failure rate remains high – anything from 40–70%, depending on whom you ask. A series of very visible outsourcing calamities at big companies like Dell and Lehman Brothers (which re-insourced helpdesks) and JP Morgan (which clawed back its IT functions) raised doubts over whether the practice had a future at all. Certain British government agencies have had a similarly dismal record with third-party IT projects. Yet outsourcing volumes keep growing, along with the categories of work involved.

It may be hard to do but it's not a complicated idea. Outsourcing is farming out a particular function, perhaps an entire process, to a third party. If you pay someone to come in and water the plants in the reception area that's outsourcing, even if it's at the easy end of the implementation scale. In concept, outsourcing has been around nearly as long as manufacturing. Contracting with a parts supplier to make components for you is outsourcing, strictly speaking, but that's not what people really mean by it. Instead, they are talking about contracting out services and processes.

timeline

1950	1960
Supply chain management	Strategic alliances

> **The number of US manufacturing jobs has fallen, but it has little to do with outsourcing and a lot to do with technological innovation.**
>
> **Walter Williams, 2005**

It all began to gather steam in the 1980s and early 1990s. Michael Porter's value chain analysis (see page 188) was gaining a following at the time, and there were the first stirrings of a strategic return to the core (see page 36). What is our core business, and where do we add value, management asked itself. The logic was that if you didn't have superior skills in a function and it didn't add value, why do it? Someone else could do it better and, probably, cheaper.

Running the canteen Computer bureaux had been an early form of outsourcing provider for those who couldn't afford computing power or time, and IT remains one of the most outsourced functions to this day. The next candidates were services like managing the company's buildings and facilities, or running the canteen. It became standard practice for the outsourcer to take on at least some of the existing staff from those departments and, if there were any assets involved, to acquire those too and pay for them.

Firms gradually developed enough confidence in the concept, and the providers, to begin handing over entire business processes, starting with payroll, data entry and insurance claims. This was 'business process outsourcing', or BPO to its friends. IT outsourcing (ITO) is a subset of BPO. The principle widened to include processes like billing, purchasing and finance – what Indian contractors call 'non-voice' work. Along a separate trajectory, it spread, notoriously, to customer relations

1970s	**1983**	**1985**	**1990**
Outsourcing	Globalization	Value chain	Core competence

❝The majority of Americans (71%) say outsourcing jobs overseas is "bad for US economy".❞

Foreign Policy Association/ Zogby International survey, 2004

management and technical support via call centres that were often located in other countries.

Some call this 'offshoring' though purists insist that the word means relocating part of your business abroad, not relinquishing ownership. Paying a call centre in Calcutta to deal with your customers is merely offshore outsourcing. Either way, it is a sensitive issue, both politically and for the people who lose their jobs – unlike domestic outsourcing, they can't cross the street for a job with the new service provider.

BPO is largely concerned with carrying out routine processes, albeit in some curious niches. One London outsourcing provider handles employees' expense claims over the Internet. So-called 'knowledge process outsourcing' – yes, KPO – farms out brainpower, in the shape of research, analysis and technical skills.

What benefits do companies expect? For those feeling the pinch, the asset sales and payroll cuts can be enough to prompt the switch, though outsourcing experts will tell you that this is a bad reason. None the less, outsourcing does lower costs, either because the provider has better economies of scale or, if the outsourced work goes offshore, through lower labour costs. Other compelling motives may include getting work done more efficiently or effectively and tighter budget control through more predictable costs.

Maintaining quality and security of information are perennial concerns for many companies, and the cost savings are not as dramatic as some anticipate, which is why they need a properly thought-out business case to justify the change. Whatever price the contract may specify, specialists say users should add 10% to set up the arrangement and manage it, and anything up to 65% if the work is going offshore, thanks to travel costs

> **❝[Outsourcing] simply says where the work can be done outside better than it can be done inside, we should do it. ❞**
>
> **Alphonso Jackson, 2003**

and the complexities of cultural alignment. Other costs may include benchmarking and analysis to check that this really is the right choice, and redundancies. The transition period – 'the valley of despair' to some insiders – can last from a few months to a couple of years and is often marked by a drop in productivity as things settle down.

Polarizing market Among suppliers of outsourcing services, the market is polarizing, as markets do, into a small number of big full-service providers at home and abroad, and a raft of smaller specialist suppliers. In time, it may evolve to provide à la carte menus of services, easier to access than today's offerings.

While India dominates the offshore market, particularly in software work, other popular destinations include Ireland, the Philippines, Russia, Poland and the Czech Republic. Yet there is already a reverse flow, with small providers popping up in rural America.

The iron rule is never to outsource strategy. That apart, is anything else beyond outsourcing's reach? Possibly not. Outsourcing's most useful contribution to the practice of management may be that it is embedding a discipline of looking at absolutely everything in the business and asking: 'Should we really be doing this?'

the condensed idea
Should we really be doing this?

37 Project management

There are more lawyers, accountants and business school graduates in top management these days, and fewer engineers. The engineer as business manager is in eclipse, along with the shrinking weight of manufacturing in developed economies. Yet there is much that managers can and do learn from the down-and-dirty business of project management, in planning complex projects and forcing them through to conclusion.

A project is very different to a process. A process carries out the same function again and again to yield a product or a service. A project is a one-off undertaking, with a clear beginning and end, usually aimed at creating some useful change or adding value – typically to build a new plant or create a new product. The skills needed to complete a project successfully are not those required to manage a process, and so project management has evolved as a discipline of its own.

Projects bring together resources such as people, money and material, and these must be organized and managed to produce a defined result. The hard part is to bring the project to completion within a specified time, at no more than a specified cost. Various tools have been created to help project managers pull off this invariably challenging feat. The most enduring were developed within the US chemical and defence industries.

The father of project management is generally regarded to be Henry Gantt, a colleague of Frederick Taylor, the creator of scientific

timeline

1911

Scientific management

management (see page 152). He is most famously remembered for the Gantt chart, a bar chart plotted against days, weeks or months that even today tells supervisors at a glance whether their project is on schedule or not. But it was not until the 1950s that two of the best known project management tools came into being – the critical path method (CPM) and the programme evaluation and review technique (PERT).

Critical path method This was devised by researchers at DuPont and Remington-Rand to manage the complex business of shutting down plants for maintenance and then restarting them. CPM begins by providing a diagramatic view of the project, showing the time required to complete each of its component activities. The diagram will then reveal which activities are critical to keeping the project on schedule – and which are not. It works like this:

1. Define the individual activities.
2. List them in the order they must be performed – some can't be started until others have been completed
3. Create an activity diagram or flowchart showing each activity in relation to the others.
4. Estimate the time needed to carry out each activity.
5. Identify the critical path. This is the route through the network – the diagram – that will take the longest amount of time. None of the activities lying along this path can be delayed without delaying the entire project.

> **'One-way communication doesn't work. You must be in two-way conversation to have people perform to the schedule. Planning is conversation.'**
> **Hal Macomber, 2002**

Tasks which are not on the critical path can fall behind schedule – up to a point – without blowing the whole project's completion date. This leeway for slippage in non-critical activities is called 'slack' or 'float'. The activities on the critical path have no slack at all. It often happens that the activity diagram reveals more than one critical path – in fact, project managers like to say that the perfectly balanced project is all critical path. Armed with a CPM diagram, project managers know how long their

Tyranny of the triangle

Projects always have constraints, and there are three major ones, forming a triangle – the 'project management triangle'. You can't change one side of the triangle without having an effect on the other two.
The three constraints are:

Time – the hardest to control

Cost – soars when time is all-important

Scope – what the project is supposed to accomplish

Juggling all three is not easy. As the cynics say:
'Pick two – good, fast or cheap.'

complex project will take to complete, and which tasks are absolutely vital to staying on schedule. In the diagram the critical path is task 1, followed by task 3 and then task 5. This gives three days' slack in the path of task 2, followed by task 4 and then task 5.

Having identified the critical path, if project managers then add in information about the cost of each activity, and the cost of speeding up each activity, they can decide whether it is worth trying to accelerate the project – and, if so, what the optimal plan might be. That all sounds promising, but CPM does have its limitations. It is a deterministic model in the sense that its outcome is predetermined by the values fed into it – in this case, the completion times of critical tasks. Change those and you change the outcome. This means that, while CPM can cope with complexity, it is best suited to routine projects with predictable completion times. One mistake can imperil the whole project. So, if completion times are less certain, PERT is a more accommodating tool.

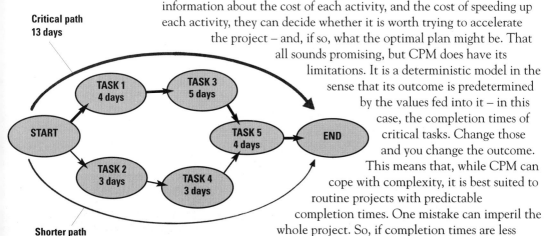

**Critical path
13 days**

START

TASK 1
4 days

TASK 3
5 days

TASK 5
4 days

END

TASK 2
3 days

TASK 4
3 days

**Shorter path
10 days**

Program evaluation and review technique PERT is a product of the US defence industry, developed by management consultants Booz Allen Hamilton in the mid-1950s for work on the Polaris nuclear submarine. It has similarities with CPM and incorporates the idea of the critical path, but it allows for randomness in the completion times of individual tasks.

Like CPM, PERT hinges on a diagram, the PERT network chart. This portrays activities, represented by lines called 'arcs', and milestones, represented by small circles called 'nodes'. Milestones (sometimes called 'events') mark the completion of an activity. The milestones are numbered sequentially in 10s – 10, 20, 30 and so on – so that new ones can be inserted without having to renumber the whole chart. The chart is drawn up in much the same way as the CPM diagram, with one key difference: the model allows three different time estimates. They are:
• Optimistic time – the shortest time in which the task can be completed, if all goes better than expected (O).
• Pessimistic time – the longest time to completion, assuming everything goes wrong (P).
• Most likely time – just that (M).

> **A two-year project will take three years; a three-year project will never finish.**
> Anon.

The project manager can then calculate the expected time, which is the average time if the task were repeated again and again over an extended period. The formula is that expected time = $(O + 4M + P)/6$.

The project's critical path is again determined by adding the times for the activities in each sequence to see which is the longest path. These are the tasks that have to be done on time if the project is to end on schedule.

As a weapon in the project management arsenal, the critical path is as important as it ever was, not least for those in the software industry. The main difference is that, while critical path calculations were once done with pencil and paper, these days a software package will do it for you.

the condensed idea
Getting it done

38 Scientific management

Is management an art or a science? The debate is not new, nor is it over. In recent times, the 'art' lobby has been making up some lost ground, but it was 19th-century engineer Frederick Winslow Taylor who first cast management as a science. Peter Drucker, the management guru's management guru, says Taylor deserves a place alongside Darwin and Freud in the making of the modern world.

Taylor believed that production was subject to universal laws that were independent of human judgement. It was the task of scientific management to uncover these laws, to discover the 'one best way' of doing things. It might be the best way of shovelling coal, of securing a bolt or of ensuring quality control. Taylor is largely forgotten outside business schools these days. When his memory surfaces, it's often for the worst of reasons. He was the first to break work down into small pieces, measure them and put them back together so they operated more efficiently. He was keen to eliminate wasted effort and invented the time and motion study. In short, he was the world's first efficiency expert, and is sometimes caricatured as the creator of all that is worst about factory life. For some – trades unionists and Marxists are prime examples – 'Taylorism' is still a dirty word that stands for an exploitative, worker-as-automaton management style. In fact, Taylor believed his

> **'This paper has been written . . . to prove that the best management is a true science, resting upon clearly defined laws, rules, and principles.'**
>
> **Frederick Winslow Taylor, 1911**

timeline

1911

Scientific management

methods would benefit workers too (and, to his credit, he did invent the smoke break and the suggestions box).

It's striking how many theories of management are generated these days by people who have never done a day's 'work' – making or selling stuff – in their lives. Modern management thinking is dominated by academics and consultants rather than managers. But Taylor hatched his theories where he meant them to apply, down on the factory floor.

Born into a well-to-do Quaker family in Pennsylvania, bad eyesight forced Taylor to abandon hopes of an academic career, and he became an apprentice patternmaker at a local steelworks instead. He studied mechanical engineering at night and eventually became the company's chief engineer. Along the way he invented several devices, modified a number of processes to make them more efficient and published a paper that elevated metal-cutting into a science.

> **❛The principal object of management should be to secure the maximum prosperity for the employer, coupled with the maximum prosperity for each employee.❜**
> **Frederick Winslow Taylor, 1911**

Many and varied Finally, he turned his attention to the workers themselves. It's probably hard to appreciate the full extent of his influence without knowing what manufacturing was like before. In those days, work was mostly carried out by skilled craftsmen who, like Taylor, had served apprenticeships. Their techniques and work patterns were as many and varied as the men themselves. Manufacturing was carried out in thousands of small shops and was, by any standard, hopelessly inefficient. Managers, such as they were, had very little contact with workers, who were managed by foremen. There was no love lost between labour and management, who often regarded each other with hostility.

Taylor could see all this, and he determined to apply the methods of science to work, and the management of work, so as to improve

1960	**1993**
Theories X & Y (and Theory Z)	BPR

Henry Ford and the assembly line

The most influential legacy of Taylorism was Fordism. Engineer Henry Ford began making his famous Model T car in 1908, priced at $950. His declared aim was to build a car for the 'great multitude' but, for the great multitude, that was too much money. Over the next five years he gradually introduced four principles to bring down the cost – continuous flow, division of labour, interchangeable parts and less wasted effort.

Inspired by Chicago's meatpacking plants and a memory of a flour mill conveyor belt, he realized that, if the work was brought to the workers on a moving line, they spent less time moving about. He used Frederick Taylor's ideas on task allocation – breaking the task into smaller tasks – and separated Model T assembly into 84 steps. And he hired Taylor to carry out time studies, to establish the pace and exact motions of the workers. The moving assembly line was finally commissioned in 1913, cutting production time per vehicle from 728 minutes to 93 minutes. When production of the Model T ceased in 1927, Ford had sold 15 million, at prices as low as $280.

productivity. One of the things he had observed in the steel industry was the way in which workers deliberately operated below their capacity. This was generally known as 'soldiering'. Taylor believed that soldiering and low productivity had various causes. Workers believed that if they worked harder, fewer of them would be needed and some would lose their jobs. The system paid the same regardless of how much each worker produced. Why work harder if you didn't have to? And the workers' 'rule-of-thumb' methods, approaching each task in their own individual way, resulted in much wasted effort.

Taylor began to experiment with ways of finding the optimum performance level for certain jobs, becoming the original man with stopwatch and clipboard. He would break a task down into its constituent elements, timing each of them to within fractions of a second, and working out the most productive routines – 'screw on this bolt in 16.4 seconds'. He called his experiments 'time studies'. Importantly, he also believed that wages should be based on performance.

Shovelling Taylor's best-known experiment looked at shovelling. He determined that the optimal weight for a worker to lift in a shovel – the weight that would keep him working longest without tiring – was 21½ lb. Materials like coal and iron ore have different densities, so the optimal shovel for each of them will be a different size. The workers were issued with optimal shovels and, as predicted, productivity shot up nearly fourfold. Pay went up accordingly – Taylor believed in paying more for greater output. But the number of shovellers was reduced from 500 to 140, so perhaps the workers were right to be suspicious.

Scientific method, he claimed, applied to 'the man at the head of the business' just as much as to the workman. 'In the past the man has been first; in the future the system must be first,' he wrote, with an Orwellian lack of irony. The four objectives of scientific management were these:
• to replace rule-of-thumb work methods with scientifically devised methods;
• to select, train and develop each worker, again scientifically, instead of leaving them to train themselves;
• to develop a spirit of cooperation between workers and management, to make sure that the scientifically worked-out methods are being followed;
• to divide work between managers and workers in almost equal shares, so that the managers plan the work scientifically and the workers perform the tasks.

Taylor laid down principles of organization, which became the forerunners of much subsequent organizational theory. They included clear delineation of authority; separation of planning from operations; incentive schemes for workers; and task specialization.

Taylor's ideas were deployed in many factories, where they duly raised productivity. Unscrupulous managers used them to cut pay and, even in more sympathetic hands, they certainly increased the monotony of work. He transformed the way work was done, however, and important elements of scientific management survive to this day. Human resources and quality control are only two of the corporate departments that have their roots in what he did.

the condensed idea
The one best way

39 Six Sigma

Martial arts mixes with the Greek alphabet and a US electronics maker in a defects control discipline that has won many thousands of corporate converts – Six Sigma. It was designed to reduce defects and shorten cycle times, something it does very effectively, but today its sponsors are promoting it as a fully integrated management system.

Six Sigma was developed in the 1980s by electronics and communications firm Motorola. It was part of that company's response to devastating competition from foreign – read 'Japanese' – manufacturers. Sales were taking a hammering and there was a rising tide of complaints from the field sales force about warranty claims. As Motorola tells the story, the senior sales vice president looked the chief executive in the eye and said: 'Our quality stinks.' The two of them agreed on a goal of tenfold quality improvement over the next ten years.

The job of making that happen fell to Bill Smith, an engineer and scientist in Motorola's communications division. He drew together a variety of existing methodologies, largely from Japanese practices, and in 1986 introduced the concept of Six Sigma. It was, the company said, 'a new method for standardizing the way defects are counted, with Six Sigma being near perfection'. As it has evolved, its aim is to achieve total customer satisfaction by delivering products on time, without defects or excessive failures in service.

Sigma is the Greek letter 'S', its lower-case form written, ironically enough, as if it were the number 6 bowing to the east. In statistical shorthand, sigma is used to represent standard deviation, a measure of how

timeline

1940s	1986
Lean manufacturing	Six Sigma

wildly a set of numbers deviate from their 'mean' or average. If the mean is an index of quality, reducing the standard deviation will reduce the number of products that fall wildly below it.

To qualify for Six Sigma status, a process must produce no more than 3.4 defective parts per million (which supposedly represents a sigma of 6). The methodology for changing processes that need incremental improvement is summed up by the acronym DMAIC, which represents the important steps in the process:

Define the problem, to determine what has to improve.
Measure the current state against the desired state.
Analyse the root cause of the gap between them.
Improve the process, by brainstorming, selecting and implementing the best solution.
Control the long-term sustainability of the improvements by establishing monitoring mechanisms, accountabilities and work tools.

To design new processes or products that will conform to Six Sigma quality, there is the DMADV methodology – define, measure analyse, design, verify. This can also be used if an existing process is performing so poorly that it needs more than incremental change.

Belted up Employees have to be trained and certified to implement Six Sigma, which has spawned a sub-industry of trainers and certifiers. Competing with them is the company's own Motorola University, which offers at-source Six Sigma training and consulting services. Maintaining the Japanese flavour, certification means becoming a green belt or black belt, something that requires on-the-job experience as well as time in the classroom. Green belts are the footsoldiers of the process improvement

> **We think about Six Sigma at three different levels: as a metric, as a methodology, as a management system. Essentially, Six Sigma is all three at the same time.**
> **Motorola University**

Sigma gets lean

Classic Six Sigma cuts defects and raises quality. Lean manufacturing (see page 112) concentrates on speed, efficiency and eliminating waste. A combination of the two has evolved to create a powerful engine for growth and profitability. Meet Lean Six Sigma.

Each of the two methodologies has something to give to the other. Six Sigma will eliminate defects, but doesn't address the question of how to optimize process flow. Lean does just that, but doesn't include the statistical tools that can minimize process variation. Lean makes work faster, and Six Sigma makes it better.

Manufacturers like BMW and Xerox have turned to Lean Six Sigma to reduce costs and complexity or to drive strategic change programmes. It is also being deployed in service industries like banking, insurance and retailing, as well as in government. The methodology can be used to link strategy to operational improvements, to create value and to build customer loyalty.

> **❝Six Sigma works within the framework of an existing process, but it does not challenge the process.❞**
>
> **Michael Hammer, 2001**

teams, and black belts – whose Motorola University course currently costs over $13,000 – are the NCOs. Black belts who demonstrate 'impact and experience' over some time may be elevated to master black belt status. They tackle the most complex improvement projects, and they coach black and green belters.

Six Sigma has had its share of bad press, and some technical purists say that its results can be distorted. Its supporters retort that it may embody some imprecision, but that this is to miss the point. It works, they say, with benefits that include greatly reduced costs and waste, faster cycle times and improved customer satisfaction. Because the way to do it is specified in such detail, it is easy, though not quick, to implement. Yet, with its culture of customer-centredness and fact-based analytics, it is clearly more than just a toolbox for manufacturing. Motorola thinks so too. By the early 1990s Six Sigma was already being used in non-manufacturing industries such as financial services, high-tech and transport. In 2002, Motorola wheeled out a new version of Six Sigma that went way beyond the factory floor, calling it 'an overarching high performance system that executes business strategy'. This new Six Sigma – Six Sigma 2.0, if you like – stipulates the following four steps:

• Align executives to the right objectives and targets, by creating a balanced scorecard (see page 8) of strategic goals, metrics and initiative. These will identify improvements that will have most effect on the bottom line.

• Mobilize improvement teams, using the DMAIC method.

• Accelerate results – change is best accomplished in sprints rather than marathons.

• Govern sustained improvement, and share best practices with those parts of the organization that can benefit.

> **You need both lean and Six Sigma . . . to drive improvements in ROIC and achieve the best competitive position.**
>
> **Michael George** (CEO George Group)

In this way, Motorola claims, companies can grow market share, improve customer retention, develop new products and services, accelerate innovation and manage changing customer requirements.

Overstretching a good idea Some have expressed scepticism about this latest development along the Six Sigma timeline. They fear that a good idea might damage its reputation – and so prevent its adoption – by making exaggerated claims about what it can realistically achieve. Much the same happened to business process reengineering (see page 24) towards the end of the 1990s.

One of those who worries that this may be happening to Six Sigma is Dr Michael Hammer who, as one of the founders of business process reengineering, should know what he is talking about. 'A Six Sigma train wreck . . . would be a tragedy for all the companies who could in fact benefit from a rational and measured application of this valuable technique,' he has said.

To avoid disaster, Hammer advised that practitioners should develop a balanced perspective on Six Sigma, recognizing that it is not the universal answer to all business problems. It is, he said, just one tool among many, very useful for a particular set of problems.

the condensed idea
Cutting defects

40 Stakeholders

It is the fate of some words to evolve rapidly through enlightening to hot, overused and, finally, very irritating, and 'stakeholder' has become one of them. It is sprinkled over reports and jammed into mission statements, as if use alone were enough to prove concern. Worse, politicians have got hold of it. In their mouths, it seems to refer to the population at large, which makes them sound caring without meaning very much. All this is a pity because its original concept represents a radical shift in the way the corporation views, or should view, itself.

The stakeholder idea began its march with R. Edward Freeman's 1984 book *Strategic Management: A Stakeholders Approach*. Freeman held that commercial firms would be much more effectively managed at a strategic level if the concerns of various stakeholders were taken into account. In other words, there would be long-term benefit for shareholders. He said later that the word 'stakeholder' was chosen deliberately to contrast with 'stockholder'. Freeman defined a stakeholder in an organization as any individual or group who 'can affect or is affected by' its activities. That's sufficiently broad to include a company's competitors, which seems unnecessarily generous. But it drew attention to the fact that companies live in a community, and that good neighbours tend to lead more fulfilled lives.

The idea caused a stir in academic circles, but it also rubbed off onto the real world of business. Further momentum came from the Caux Round Table, a group of business people from Europe, North America and Japan who first gathered in Switzerland to try to find an escape from

timeline

1970	1984
Corporate social responsibility	Stakeholders

international trade tensions. Along the way, the group recognized that big companies had a global responsibility to reduce social and economic threats to world peace and stability and, in 1994, it issued the first code of international business ethics – the Caux Principles (see box) – principles of 'stakeholder management'.

Flesh on the bones A year later, an extraordinary, networked five-year project began, involving several hundred scholars from all over the world. It was called *Redefining the Corporation*, was supported by a grant from the Alfred P. Sloan Foundation, and looked at the stakeholder model of the corporation and its implications for management theory, research and business practice. In 2002 academics James E. Post, Lee E. Preston and Sybille Sachs published the project's final book under the same name. It calls for business to rethink its purpose and, drawing on the experiences of Cummings Engine Company, Motorola and Shell (including the notorious Brent Spar affair – see page 47), fleshes out the concept of the stakeholder.

> **The [Japanese] concept of *kyosei* – working together for the common good – is broadly consistent with a stakeholder view of the corporation.**
>
> **James E. Post, Lee E. Preston and Sybille Sachs,** 2002

The authors don't see the firm as being one entity and stakeholders another – the corporation is a 'collaboration of multiple and diverse constituencies and interests referred to as stakeholders'. Their main thesis is that specific stakeholder relationships go beyond enlightened self-interest. They are central to the creation (or destruction) of 'organizational wealth' and, as such, to the core purposes and operations of the corporation. So stakeholder management, defined as managing relationships with stakeholders for mutual benefit, is critical to corporate success.

'Corporations *are* what they *do*', the authors claim. Firms clearly no longer conform to the medieval model, whose social purpose was central. Nor should they conform to the current 'ownership' model that puts the heaviest emphasis on the private interests of investors. The purpose of the

Stakeholders in principle

The *Redefining the Corporation* project has drawn up seven principles of stakeholder management.

1. Managers should acknowledge and actively monitor the concerns of all legitimate stakeholders, and should take their interests appropriately into account in decision-making and operations.

2. Managers should listen to and openly communicate with stakeholders about their respective concerns and contributions, and about the risks that they assume because of their involvement with the corporation.

3. Managers should adopt processes and modes of behaviour that are sensitive to the concerns and capabilities of each stakeholder constituency.

4. Managers should recognize the interdependence of efforts and rewards among stakeholders, and should attempt to achieve a fair distribution of the benefits and burdens of corporate activity among them, taking into account their respective risks and vulnerabilities.

5. Managers should work cooperatively with other entities, both public and private, to insure that risks and harms arising from corporate activities are minimized and, where they cannot be avoided, appropriately compensated.

6. Managers should avoid altogether activities that might jeopardize inalienable human rights (e.g. the right to life) or give rise to risks which, if clearly understood, would be patently unacceptable to relevant stakeholders.

7. Managers should acknowledge the potential conflicts between (a) their own role as corporate stakeholders, and (b) their legal and moral responsibilities for the interests of stakeholders, and should address these through open communication, appropriate reporting and incentive systems and, where necessary, third party review.

corporation is to create wealth, but its legitimacy – its social charter or 'licence to operate' – depends on its ability to meet the expectations of a large group of constituents. The connection between wealth and responsibility has been acknowledged for more than a century and, if the corporation is to survive, they insist, it must adapt to social change. The authors claim there are two reasons why there is a need to redefine the large corporation. One is its sheer size and power, and the other that, while shareholders hold securities, they don't actually own the company in any meaningful sense – and they are certainly not the only constituents vital to its success. By their nature, major multinationals alter the social, political and physical environments in which they operate, and these impacts have to be thought of as part of their output. Output is the responsibility of a firm's managers and, sometimes, it can be unwanted or even harmful. Rather than attracting costly, unwanted and possibly ineffective government intervention, managers can reduce these effects if they are motivated to do so.

Ditching the conventional ownership model doesn't mean 'the death of property rights', however, or 'the end of shareholder value' (both criticisms of the stakeholder model). As early as 1946, Peter Drucker described as a 'crude old legal fiction' the idea that the company was nothing but the sum of the property rights of the shareholders. Post, Preston and Sachs say there is a similarity and mutuality of interests among the corporation's constituents, and that it cannot survive if it doesn't take responsibility for their welfare and the well-being of the society within which it operates.

A stake in the game The point of the stakeholder definition is that they have a stake in the outcome of the game, and want the corporation to be run in such a way that it makes them better off or at least, no worse off. In *Toward a Stakeholder Theory of the Firm*, Thomas Kochan and Saul Rubinstein isolate three stakeholder ID tags: they supply critical resources; their welfare is affected by the fate of the enterprise; or they have power to affect its performance, favourably or unfavourably.

By either measure, stakeholders include employees, investors, customers, unions, suppliers, regulators, local communities and citizens, various private organizations and governments. Benefits or harms between them and the firm flow both ways, according to Post, Preston and Sachs – even involuntary stakeholders, like those living near a factory, contribute by tolerating the presence of the firm and receive benefits or harms as a result. They can be linked to each other as well as to the firm, and may be at each other's throats over an issue. Communities are like that.

> **❛The stakeholders in a corporation are the individuals and constituencies that contribute, either voluntarily or involuntarily, to its wealth-creating capacity and activities, and that are therefore its potential beneficiaries and/or risk bearers.❜**
> **Jams E. Post, Lee E. Preston and Sybille Sachs, 1984**

the condensed idea
We're all in this together

41 Strategic alliances

'It's partner or perish', declared Xerox CEO Anne Mulcahy. She was announcing yet another in the chain of strategic alliances that her company has built, to powerful effect, over many years, starting with Fuji of Japan in 1960. It may have sounded like roll-of-the-drums hyperbole, but in today's fast-moving markets – and particularly in the high-tech arena where Xerox competes – it was no more than a reasonable observation.

Managers and shareholders want their businesses to grow, though not always for the same reasons. Growth comes from building share in existing markets or expanding into new ones, and there is more than one way of doing either. The conventional options have always been either to build growth, or to buy it. Companies can grow organically, the hard, backbreaking way. The (deceptively) easy alternative is go out and acquire a competitor or a business in the chosen new market. The trouble with acquisition is that it is expensive, risky and, when it comes to post-merger integration, exhausting.

> **'The ability to attract partners and manage alliances . . . is the new core competency of the networked age.'**
>
> **Matt Schifrin, 2001**
> (editor Forbes.com)

Buying without paying 'Strategic alliances' can provide many of the benefits of acquisition without too many of the problems, more quickly and at a fraction of the cost. Some companies prefer to call it 'partnering'. Whatever you call it, a strategic alliance is an agreement between two or more organizations to pool resources to achieve common goals. They can be established between complementary firms, with customers or suppliers,

timeline

1450	1916
Innovation	Diversification

Alliance calling

Japan's mobile Internet market is dominated by NTT DoCoMo's i-mode service, which has seized over 50% of it. Alliances are central to the way i-mode's offering has appealed to users. In what's known as an 'orchestrator' strategy, it built a series of partnerships with content providers well before its launch.

The rich mix of content and services, with pride of place on the handset menu, immediately struck a chord with consumers, giving i-mode the benefit of an alluring offering. The partners get traffic and other pluses. DoCoMo charges a small fee for each site visit and hands most of it to the content provider. They also share DoCoMo's research into subscriber usage patterns.

Alliances have also been the vehicle for i-mode's international expansion, which is improving economies of scale in the production of i-mode standard handsets. It has partnered with nine local telecom operators in Europe to create a continent-wide i-mode network. The next step will be to use i-mode as a platform for delivering financial services. More alliances . . .

with competitors (on a carefully defined basis), academic and research establishments or even government agencies. Alliances are generally motivated by something more specific than brute growth, though that will usually be the ultimate aim. It may be the need for access to a particular technology or intellectual property. It may be a way of establishing a presence in a particular territory or acquiring a new distribution channel. Broadening the product range for existing customers, cutting research and development costs or reducing time-to-market are other reasons.

In nearly all of the above, a carefully structured alliance should reduce risk. Rather appealingly, alliances also provide access to a partner's capital. Indeed, some business advisers refer to them as 'virtual funding' because they bring all the benefits associated with a cash injection, relatively quickly and without having to borrow money or sell more shares.

1960	1970s	1990	2004
Strategic alliances	Outsourcing	Core competence	Web 2.0

With all that going for them, strategic alliances have been multiplying in recent years, to the point where they now outnumber mergers and acquisitions in terms of how many take place each year. In simple marketing alliances, firms exchange customer data and sell to each other's client base – you might earn royalties on their sales to your customers.

In a product alliance, you offer another company's goods to your own customers, expanding your range without costly investment. These and more complex know-how exchanges are especially prevalent in technology and IT industries, where rapid access to new products and research is vital in order to remain competitive.

> **This drive to equity-based alliances amounts to a new chapter in the evolution of free enterprise.**
> **Peter Pekar and Marc Margulis, 2003**

This acceleration in partnering is partly driven by a cooling of enthusiasm for the good old-fashioned merger (for which, read 'takeover'). It is becoming common currency that more mergers fail than succeed, and that any positive shareholder value is more likely to accrue to sellers rather than buyers. In competitive auctions, the winner is inclined to overpay, invoking what they call 'the winner's curse'. Any management with its eye on the stock price will see attractions in the alliance alternative.

Alliance mania is also a product of the growing complexity and speed of today's business environment. Companies are bombarded with threats and opportunities, but their capacity to respond is limited by finite capital and human resources. On the one hand, they are beckoned by crumbling geographical and technological barriers. On the other, many have retreated into their core competencies (see page 36) and need partners if they are going to venture out again.

A range of options The strategic alliance is one of a range of corporate alliance options that demand different degrees of partner commitment and integration. At one end is licensing, an alliance of a kind, but usually a contractual arrangement involving little actual collaboration. Next comes the non-equity alliance, which shares resources but stops short of exchanging equity. Commitment must be more intense in equity alliances, of which there are two types. The first involves partial acquisition, where one party acquires shares in the other, or cross-equity arrangements where they take minority stakes in each other.

The second, most integrated form of equity alliance is the joint venture, where the partners set up a new company in which they each have an interest. These take longer to set up, can be complicated to manage and may take up quite a lot of senior management time.

Some of the most successful alliances have come together to accomplish very specific goals. US telecoms group BellSouth partnered with Dutch telco KPN to drive into the German mobile phone market, while Nestlé and Häagen Dazs joined up to compete with Unilever in the US ice cream market.

Ending in tears In business, as in life, intimate relationships don't always run smoothly. In the early 1990s, Apple and IBM formed a strategic alliance to develop a next-generation microcomputer operating system. Called Taligent, it faded away quietly. An automobile industry alliance between Honda and Rover ended in tears.

Organizations have learnt from others' mistakes and the odds on success have improved, as long as basic rules are followed. Know exactly what you want from the partnership and why you are entering it. Find the right partner through diligent research – if alliance is a recovery strategy, a partner in as much trouble as you is unlikely to solve your problem. Be crystal clear on what each partner expects of the other, and get a good lawyer to write it down.

Some alliances find that an exchange of people helps to build necessary trust and understanding between the partners. Specialize, letting each partner do what it does best. And remember, it doesn't have to go on forever. Alliances should last only while they are useful to both partners. Once the goal is achieved, they should be allowed to lapse without rancour. That's why some say many strategic alliances would be better labelled 'tactical alliances'. But it doesn't sound quite as grand.

the condensed idea
New markets with less risk

42 Supply chain management

When supply chain managers compare notes, the talk will eventually get round to 'the perfect order'. That's an order which reached the customer complete, in the right place, undamaged and on time. Like other manifestations of perfection, it is not as common as some companies would like. Lower-than-necessary perfect order rates not only create unhappy customers, but suggest supply chain inefficiencies that are costing the company money. So attention to the supply chain has moved out of warehouses and loading bays and into Mahogany Row.

The supply chain is made up of the physical and information links between suppliers and the company on one side, and the company and its customers on the other. It includes production planning, purchasing, materials handling and, under the subset of 'logistics', transport and storage (warehouses and distribution centres). Though companies used to think of the supply side and the demand (customer) side as two separate strands, today they increasingly regard them, and manage them, as one continuous chain. For many years, it was the chain from their suppliers that preoccupied manufacturers most. The route to the customer was the distribution channel (see page 32), a problem that belonged to a different part of the company.

The history of the supplier end of the chain was written largely by the big motor companies, for whom it has always been a crucial issue. In the early

timeline

1940s	1950
Lean manufacturing	Supply chain management

days, Ford manufactured most of its components itself, so suppliers were not a huge consideration. General Motors 'outsourced' parts manufacture in 1920 (see page 144), but only to its own subsidiaries. It wasn't until 1950 that Ford began to outsource in the true sense, to other companies, and it was then that the tricky supply chain business of delivery dates, quantities, inventory, quality and breakages began to arise.

> **'Supply chain is no longer a back-office activity. It has become a potential competitive weapon in the boardroom.'**
>
> **Kevin O'Connell,** 2005
> (IBM integrated supply chain division)

In those days, if you had too many supplies, you simply stored them in a warehouse until they were needed – rather have too much than run out, was the attitude. But holding stocks – inventory – ties up money. You have paid for it and there it sits, idle. Until the stocks are incorporated in a product and sold, the working capital they represent is non-productive. The same applies to finished products gathering dust in a warehouse. You have laid out more money than if you had planned the inventory flow better, and the surplus could be sitting in a bank, earning interest, or being spent on something more useful. So inventory is a cost – reduce it and you save money. Managers of old might have gazed on a bulging warehouse with pride. For today's managers, if they have any sense, it's with despair.

Just in time Learning from the Japanese, large manufacturers began to slash inventory in the 1980s by arranging for deliveries to arrive just as they were needed – 'just in time'. This meant cooperating more closely with suppliers, who have come to be regarded by smart firms as partners or stakeholders (see page 160), with whom their fortunes are closely intertwined. In sophisticated industries, the old days of hammering down the suppliers and picking the one with the lowest price are all but gone. Price remains a vital part of the mix, but no longer the only one.

If companies are running the supply side more efficiently, they have less control over the demand side. Produce too many products and you're stuck with the inventory curse. Produce too few and it's 'out of stock' – words

early 1950s		**1970s**	**1984**	**1985**
Channel management		Outsourcing	Stakeholders	Value chain

Never again

Between 2003 and 2004 the demand for cellular phone chips rose by 37%, as people around the world developed more of a taste for mobile phones. The spike in demand caught chipset-maker Qualcomm flatfooted. It was unable to fill all the orders that came flooding through because it couldn't get its hands on enough chips. Incensed, it reorganized its supply chain so that this would never happen again. Until then, Qualcomm had split its supply chain planning in two – with separate planning groups for supply and for demand. It merged them. Qualcomm also realized that, to increase its order fulfilment rates, it

needed a longer-term demand forecast that took into account just how much its suppliers were able to produce. It has upgraded its demand-planning software and now holds regular planning sessions that bring together supply chain, finance, IT, and sales and marketing. It has increased the flexibility of the supply chain by using more suppliers, with whom it now shares more information than before. And if another spike comes along unexpectedly, it can shift production back and forth between suppliers. On-time product delivery rate has risen from under 90% to 96% – high for its industry.

that strike a chill into a salesperson's heart. That's why accurate sales forecasts are so important, not so that the company can congratulate itself on a good month, but so that it can ensure it has matching levels of production – not too much, not too little.

Forecasts are notoriously unreliable, however, and customer demand can rise or fall for any number of unexpected reasons. The effects of fluctuations in real demand reach all the way back down the chain to the supplier, which needs to know promptly whether to raise or lower its own production or keep it the way it is.

Integration That's why much supply chain talk these days is also about 'integration', creating information systems that will flash messages of shifts in sales back to the company and its suppliers as soon as possible. Consumer goods manufacturers are getting better at this. With Procter & Gamble's (P&G's) old supply chain model, gaps on the retailer's shelves could take weeks to fill. Point-of-sale data collection systems at the checkout were

> **Getting our supply chain in order is 75% process and 25% tools and technologies.**
>
> **Norm Fjeldheim, 2005** (Qualcomm)

used to trigger a message to P&G's distribution centre when a certain number of products had been sold, and they would then be replenished. This could take time. Now the system informs P&G's supplier directly of every sold item on a daily basis. The empty shelf situation is much improved.

That's all very well in highly industrialized domestic markets, but globalization has added another dimension entirely. When a US firm manufactures a mobile phone in China and sells it to a retailer in Austria, the supply chain is stretched to breaking point, and sometimes beyond. There are so many links in the chain, including transport, that things are more likely to go wrong. And fancy information systems still have little effect on a supplier in some remote places, where a phone and fax is as good as it gets.

The links in the supply chain represent many of the links in Michael Porter's value chain (see page 188) and there are cost savings to be had in every one, from managing inventory to drivers' waiting time. For companies whose real business is not moving boxes of parts around the globe, there are others who can do it more efficiently, and the supply chain manager's third favourite topic of conversation is outsourcing. Today, a growing number of manufacturers outsource every link in the logistics chain. The woman on the forklift truck, driving the crate of ball bearings around the factory floor, probably doesn't work for the car company but for a specialized logistics provider. The supply chain can be a source of competitive advantage, and that's how far some companies will go to achieve it.

the condensed idea
Polishing the chain from supplier to customer

43 Systems thinking

Some farmers discovered systems thinking the hard way. With their crops being devoured by insects, they reached for the spray gun and blasted them with pesticide. And it worked – for a time. But then the crop damage returned, worse than ever, and the pesticide that was so successful had no more effect. As it happened, the insect that was eating the crops had also been eating, or competing with, another insect. Now that insect no. 1 was out of the way, insect no. 2 was having a field day. 'Systems thinking' says that things are more complicated than they seem and actions can have unforeseen and unintended consequences.

> **The concept of a system contradicts the belief that people are entirely free agents.**
>
> **Jay W. Forrester, 1998**

Systems thinking recognizes that no man – or insect – is an island, and that there is an interconnectedness in social and natural processes that is not always immediately apparent. 'Linear' thinking operates in a straight line. It says that if you do A to B, the result will be C. Systems thinking says that if you do A to B, it may also influence D and E, resulting in F – except that F may take some time to show up.

Systems thinking comes out of 'system dynamics', the child of American computer engineer Jay Forrester. He studied how even simple systems could behave in a surprisingly nonlinear way, publishing a paper on 'Industrial dynamics' in 1958. More recently, Peter Senge (see page 118) has looked at the way systems thinking and systems awareness can help people work together more productively towards common goals, in learning organizations.

timeline

1958	1985
Systems thinking	Value chain

Futuristic design

You wouldn't dream of sending a spacecraft to the moon without testing prototypes and simulating trajectories. You wouldn't even make a new electric kettle without a few lab tests. So why do we launch companies without first testing their design?

Jay Forrester, father of system dynamics, has been using computers to model social systems for years and thinks it's time we did it for real. Let's simulate and test the design of social systems (e.g. companies) to see if they work. He accepts that people dislike the idea of 'designing' social organizations, but says we have always designed them, only

badly. He says: 'Organizations built by committee and intuition perform no better than would an airplane built by the same methods'.

Real airplanes are designed by designers and flown by pilots. But in business the plane is designed by the pilots. In the future, Forrester predicts, management schools will train enterprise designers, and not just corporation operators: 'Correct design can make a corporation less vulnerable . . . Correct design can avoid the adoption of policies offering short-term advantage at the expense of long-term failure.'

Forming a circle Systems thinking sees a process as a system, not as a straight line but as a **loop** or series of interconnected loops. The system links people, institutions, processes, and so on, but they themselves are not the point – the point is the influences they have on each other. Senge argues that the roots of the 'war on terror' lie not in rival ideologies but in a way of thinking shared by both sides.

The linear thinking of the US establishment is that terrorist attacks cause a threat to Americans, which causes a need to respond militarily. Terrorist thinking says US military activity causes a perception of US aggressiveness which makes people willing to become terrorists. In fact, those two straight lines form a circle, a system of variables that influence each other – a perpetual cycle of aggression. 'Both sides respond to perceived threats', Senge says. 'But their actions end up creating escalating danger for everyone. Here, as in many systems, doing the obvious thing does not produce the obvious, desired outcome.'

> **'Feedback processes . . . are the fundamental basis for all change.'**
> Jay W. Forrester, 1998

How often could you say the same about problem-solving in the workplace? A key idea in systems thinking is 'feedback' which, confusingly, is a very different thing from the feedback you might want to obtain from the customer. Instead, it's the flow of influence between each player in the system. Every influence is both a cause and an effect. The disappearance of insect no. 1 was the effect of pesticide application and the cause of a resurgence of insect no. 2. This chain of cause and effect eventually creates a loop.

Reinforcing feedback causes escalation, and small doses of it can amplify into large results, for better or worse – the vicious circle. Self-fulfilling prophecies are examples of reinforcing feedback at work, and so is escalating tension between the US government and terrorists. **Balancing feedback** acts to stabilize the system and is the result of goal-oriented behaviour. If you are travelling at 60 miles per hour but want to drive at 50, that desire will 'influence' you to apply the brakes. If you're travelling at 40, it will cause you to put your foot down, but only until you reach 50. That's an explicit balancing feedback system. Implicit balancing feedback may be the reason why trying to change the system resists all your efforts. **Delays**, another key idea, are often present in feedback, interrupting the flow of causes or influences so that consequences only appear gradually.

> **'System dynamics arose from seeking a better understanding of management.'**
> Jay W. Forrester, 1998

You can spot systems dynamics at work in many guises, including the way in which a solution turns into a problem somewhere else in the system. A new manager 'solves' the problem of high inventory costs by reducing stocks, but the sales force ends up spending more time dealing with customers upset over late deliveries. Or sales are way down in the fourth quarter, because of the huge success of the discount programme in the third, prompting customers to bring forward their purchases. Senge tells of how the seizure of a large narcotics shipment caused a new wave of street crime by reducing the drug supply, which pushed up prices, which in turn drove desperate addicts to more crime to keep funding their habit.

Pushing back Reinforcing feedback takes place when managers' expectations influence their subordinates' performance. You think someone has high potential, so you take special care to help them develop it. They do. You feel you were right all along and help them some more. It happens in reverse, with poor performers 'justifying' lack of attention. 'The harder you push, the harder the system pushes back' is how Senge describes a typical balancing feedback system. He tells of a friend who tried in vain to reduce burnout among the professionals working for his busy training business, shortening the hours, locking the offices. No good. They took work home, defied the shortened hours, and why? The reason it happened was because an unwritten norm was that the organization's true heroes, the ones that got ahead, worked 70 hours a week – because that was the example the boss had set himself.

> **❛Reality is made up of circles but we see straight lines.❜**
> **Peter Senge,** 1990

These are simple cases. Systems within big organizations can be much more complex. Businesses have powerful and sophisticated forecasting, planning and analysis tools at their disposal and yet these fail to detect the causes of some of the most trying problems. That, says Senge, is because they are designed to handle the kind of complexity that has many variables – detail complexity. But there is another kind, which the tools are not designed to cope with – dynamic complexity – where cause and effect are subtle and the effects of interventions over time are not obvious.

Dealing with this demands a 'shift of mind', Senge declares. The essence of systems thinking, he says, is to see interrelationships rather than linear cause–effect chains, and to see processes of change rather than just snapshots.

the condensed idea
Be aware of the
interconnectedness of things

44 Theories X & Y (and Theory Z)

Management's ideas about motivating employees have changed a bit since scientific management first considered how to make workers more efficient. Today, most managers would at least pay lip service to the idea that employees are human beings, with human needs and aspirations, and that you need to recognize this to get the best from them. This may seem obvious today, but as a management precept it owes much to Douglas McGregor and his Theory X and Theory Y.

Theory X and Theory Y are a double act – a Mr Nasty and Mr Nice of human resource management – that leave you in no doubt as to which McGregor prefers, even though he insists that the optimal management style should draw from both. McGregor believed that the way a company was managed reflected its managers' view of human nature. His theories look at how satisfying the needs of employees can be used to motivate them, though each makes very different assumptions about what those needs may be. Both draw on an earlier theory of human psychology put forward in 1943 by American psychologist Abraham Maslow, known as Maslow's hierarchy of needs.

According to this theory, there is an ascending pecking order of needs, each of which – Maslow says – must be fulfilled before we can attend to the one above it. They start with physical needs and reach a peak in what he called 'self-actualization'. Starting at the bottom, they are as follows. **Physiological** – what we need simply to stay alive (air, water, food and sleep). **Safety** – once survival is assured, we need to be free from harm (to live in a safe place, have a secure job and have enough money). **Social** – with life and safety boxes ticked, social needs start to become important (we need friends, a sense of belonging, to give and receive love and to have sex). **Esteem** – having satisfied the need to belong, we want to feel important and respected. Maslow split esteem needs into two types: internal (self-esteem or a sense of achievement) and external (social status, the attention of others or reputation). In later versions of his model, Maslow added a level between esteem needs and self-actualization, acknowledging a need for knowledge and beauty – cognitive and aesthetic needs. **Self-actualization** – the apex of the pyramid and one which, unlike lower-level needs, is never satisfied. This is the instinctive need to reach your full potential – to see meaning and truth in the world – to experience harmony.

> **[The challenge is]** . . . **to innovate, to discover new ways of organizing and directing human effort, even though we recognize that the perfect organization, like the perfect vacuum, is practically out of reach.**
> **Douglas McGregor,** 1960

Enter Douglas McGregor. His 1960 book, *The Human Side of Enterprise*, set out two contrasting theories on employee motivation. He named them simply Theory X and Theory Y.

Theory X This assumes that people:
• dislike work and will avoid it if they can;
• have to be controlled and threatened before they will work hard;
• don't want responsibility and prefer to be directed;
• want to feel secure at work.

People in Theory X work only to satisfy physiological and safety needs – for money and security. The manager's role is to structure the work and incentivize the employee with pay and benefits. McGregor pointed out that Theory X was flawed because, once those needs are satisfied, they no longer motivate. And because employees have to seek to satisfy their higher-level needs outside work, their only source of continued job satisfaction will be to keep asking for more money. None the less,

1960		**1981**	**1982**
Theories X & Y (and Theory Z)		Japanese management	Organizational excellence

Herzberg on hygiene

What motivates employees is a well-trodden research path. What turns them off is less so, and one of the first to venture down it was American psychologist Frederick Herzberg. He developed his Motivation–Hygiene theory, sometimes called the Two Factor theory, which claimed that the factors causing dissatisfaction were entirely unconnected to those that gave job satisfaction. Those that satisfied he called 'motivators', and those that dissatisfied, 'hygiene factors'.

Motivators
- achievement
- work itself
- advancement
- recognition
- responsibility
- growth

Hygiene factors
- company policy
- relationship with boss
- relationship with peers
- supervision
- working conditions
- salary

Herzberg insisted that the two feelings were not opposites. The opposite of satisfaction, he said, was not dissatisfaction but *no* satisfaction. Hygiene factors cause dissatisfaction but addressing them positively would not actually motivate – just cease to dissatisfy. Motivator factors are intrinsic to the job, but the factors that affect dissatisfaction are external. Herzberg called them KITA (kick in the ass) factors, meaning they involved incentives or the threat of punishment.

Herzberg's advice was to enrich the job. It should be challenging enough to engage the full abilities of the employee and those who showed increasing levels of ability should be given more responsibilty. If the job can't use all the employee's abilities, automate or hire someone less skilled.

McGregor thought that Theory X was more practicable in large-scale production operations than Theory Y.

Theory Y This treats workers rather more like adults, and assumes that they:
- actually want to work;
- can be self-directing in line with the firm's aims, if they are committed;
- will be committed if motivated by rewards addressing their higher needs;
- can accept responsibility and may even actively seek it;
- are imaginative and creative and can use their ingenuity to solve problems at work.

According to Theory Y, the company has many more options to energize its employees. It can decentralize and delegate, spreading decision-making power among more staff. Job specifications can be broadened – like delegation, this will feed esteem needs. Employees can be consulted and included in the decision-making process, harnessing their creativity as well as giving them some control over their working lives. The resulting motivation should be considerably more galvanizing than Theory X, because it allows employees to satisfy their higher-level needs while at work.

McGregor felt that Theory Y was best suited to professional services and knowledge workers, and was particularly conducive to participative problem solving. Its ideas are sometimes collectively referred to as 'soft' management, leaving Theory X as the 'hard' variety. Others have called the styles 'participative' vs 'authoritarian'. Experimentation has revealed Theory Y to be inflexible, but much of its spirit has been absorbed by later management concepts, such as 'empowerment'. While McGregor's experience was with American companies, a British and European audience had little difficulty in seeing their own corporate structures reflected in his work. But there was a third managerial model, as the West became uncomfortably aware during the 1980s – the Japanese model.

> **❝Man is a perpetually wanting animal.❞**
> **Abraham Maslow, 1943**

The apparently unstoppable rise of Japanese industry and finance drew envious attention to their corporate structures and practices – very different to those in the West. Japanese companies offered lifetime employment, collective decision-making, implicit rather than explicit control mechanisms and an all-round concern for the employee's well-being. While this clearly resulted in a committed and highly motivated workforce, it was all so un-Western that imitation seemed out of the question.

Theory Z In 1980, however, Hawaiian-born William Ouchi published his *Theory Z: How American Management Can Meet the Japanese Challenge*. He proposed a model that combined the best of American and Japanese practices – providing lifetime employment and holistic care for employee and family, but with individual responsibilities and a mixture of explicit and implicit control mechanisms. The result, according to Dr Ouchi, should be stable employment, high productivity and high morale.

the condensed idea
What makes workers tick

45 Tipping point

The combative former US Secretary of Defense Donald Rumsfeld famously used the term 'tipping point' to describe the position that the Iraq war had not yet reached. On his and many, many other lips, 'tipping point' has passed its own tipping point, and business has leapt aboard the bandwagon.

A quick dance around the Web reveals the term – usually prefaced by 'Have we reached the . . .' – applied to the Iraq war, opinion on the Iraq war, the Afghanistan war, online media, oil, various proprietary brands of software, online advertising, online video and autism. It also shows that a surprising number of businesses have hijacked it as a trading name, including advertising agencies, marketing agencies, training companies and, bizarrely, an IT security business.

> **The world – much as we want it to – does not accord with our intuition.**
>
> **Malcolm Gladwell, 2000**

It was coined by US political scientist Morton Grodzins, who studied neighbourhood integration in the late 1950s. He found that white families would stay for a while after the first few black families moved in, but the arrival of 'one too many' caused sudden and mass white flight. That moment was the tipping point. In 2000, the principle was dressed up in new clothes by New Yorker journalist Malcolm Gladwell in his book of the same name. The subtitle unveils its theme – *How Little Things Can Make a Big Difference*.

Gladwell begins with the story of how, in the mid-1990s, Hush Puppies crepe-soled shoes leapt from being strictly for trainspotters to the hottest

timeline

fashion item in town, raising annual sales from 30,000 to 430,000 in a year. What marketer wouldn't like to have some of that? But it had nothing to do with marketing. In a spirit of inverted cool, a few hip Manhattan kids started wearing them precisely because they were so deeply unfashionable. Isaac Mizrahi, a well-known designer, began wearing them. Another designer used them in his spring collection, then another, and before long one of Hollywood's most fashionable stores had a 25-foot inflatable basset hound – the puppy in Hush Puppies – on its roof. A tipping point had been reached, and all by word of mouth or, in this case, infectious imitation.

Infectious is the word. Gladwell calls this sudden avalanche of enthusiasm an epidemic and, in fact, tipping points are a very real phenomenon in epidemiology. The difference between a viral infection dying away and flaring, in an exponential spiral, into an epidemic is very small in terms of the numbers of people who are passing on the virus. That can explain what happened to Hush Puppies. But how did it happen? Gladwell offers three reasons: the Law of the Few; the Stickiness Factor; and the Power of Context.

Three champions The Law of the Few says that for a message to spread like an epidemic it needs three kinds of people to champion it:

1. Connectors – those people who seem to know everyone, and operate across many different social sets. These are people specialists, social glue.

> **Paul Revere was a Connector.**
> **Malcolm Gladwell, 2000**

2. Mavens – people who amass knowledge in a particular subject and love to share it. They're the kind of people who can remember prices from ten years ago, know everything about sound systems or write to the newspaper. They're information specialists, human data banks.

1968	**2004**
Adhocracy	Web 2.0
	Blue ocean strategy

Have you heard . . . ?

Wanting to raise awareness of diabetes and breast cancer among the black community of San Diego, nurse Georgia Sadler set up seminars in churches around the city. Few came, and those who did were already aware and just wanted to know more. No tipping point in view, Sadler needed a context, a messenger and some stickiness and she didn't have very much money to spend.

Then she had a positively inspired idea, and moved her campaign out of the churches and into the hairdressing salon. She trained a group of stylists from around the city, using a folklorist to teach them to give information by telling stories, and then she let them loose. They had the perfect captive audience, as well as a special relationship with their clients and, like most hairdressers, they were natural conversationalists. They were Connectors, Salesmen and Mavens all in one.

Sadler fed her hairdressers with a constant stream of new conversation starters, information and titbits. Gradually, more women started to have mammograms and diabetes tests. It worked. 'Starting epidemics requires concentrating resources on a few key areas,' Malcolm Gladwell notes, 'it is possible to do a lot with a little.'

3. Salespeople – people who have what it takes, whatever that is, to convince you to try something. These are the persuaders.

The Stickiness Factor is harder to define, but it's often something quirky about the way it was delivered that makes people pay close attention to an idea or a product. Gladwell maintains *Sesame Street*, the TV programme, demonstrably improved millions of children's reading because the Muppets made it sticky. The Power of Context means the moment and the environment must be right, or no tipping power. In the crime-ridden New York City of the early 1990s, the crime rate tipped – murders fell by over 60% in five years and overall crime halved. It was thanks to a shrewd and resourceful police chief and the original message was spread not by people but by the cleanup of graffiti on the subway system. The context, powerful indeed, was that the people of the city had finally had enough.

Gladwell believes that groups can play a role in the context effect. Rebecca Wells's *Divine Secrets of the Ya-Ya Sisterhood* sold 2.5 million copies thanks largely to its adoption by women's book groups. Being in a group affects people's behaviour – films are always funnier or more thrilling when the movie theatre is full. Group conclusions are often rather different to those that would be reached by individual group members on their own. Gladwell says that, as with *Ya-Ya*, close-knit groups have the power to magnify the epidemic potential of an idea. But how big can a group become before it starts to lose cohesion, and are there lessons here for companies?

Dunbar's number Research and experience suggests a magic maximum of 150 people – sometimes known as Dunbar's number – is the largest group with whom anyone can maintain stable relationships. British anthropologist Robin Dunbar came up with this limit having studied primates as well as prehistoric tribe and village sizes. Settlements of Hutterites, the communal Anabaptist sect, traditionally split when they reach 150. At WL Gore Associates, makers of Gore-Tex, when a plant has 150 people in it the company opens a new one. Gore has been highly profitable for nearly 40 years and ranks high, if not top, in 'best places to work' lists in the US, UK, Germany, Italy and the European Union as a whole.

Gladwell believes Gore has created 'an organized mechanism that makes it much easier for new ideas and information to tip' – in other words, to go from one person or part of the group to the whole group all at once, exploiting the bonds of memory and peer pressure: 'Were Gore to try to reach each employee singly, their task would have been much harder.'

> **The theory of Tipping Points requires . . . that we reframe the way we think about the world.**
>
> **Malcolm Gladwell, 2000**

Gladwell has been mobbed as an instant management guru, and has joined the lecture circuit, though he insists he remains committed to his journalism. Though some accuse him of merely stating the obvious, he has been admired by management theorists as eminent as Henry Mintzberg (see page 4). W. Chan Kim and Renée Mauborgne (see page 16) were sufficiently drawn by his ideas to write 'Tipping point leadership', a detailed case study of New York's crime-busting project.

the condensed idea
Little things can make a big difference

46 Total quality management

If management is a science, as some have argued, it is an imprecise one and one which encourages an endless flow of management ideas that surface and then, as often as not, sink. Where there has been truly impressive progress is in the realm of quality, where science and maths feel quite at home. Much of the science has come from Americans. But there has been a lot of human insight too, and that has often come from Japan.

This powerful combination first reached many Western companies during the early 1980s in the form of 'total quality management' (TQM). This was a synthesis of different ideas and tools that had evolved in Japan since the Second World War. One of its principal architects was a former US census statistician called W. Edwards Deming, who was summoned to Japan in 1947 by the Supreme Command of the Allied occupying powers. They wanted him to do something about the poor levels of Japanese quality – all too apparent in their locally sourced supplies.

> **'Transformation is everybody's job.'**
> **W. Edwards Deming, 1986**

Deming took Japanese industry in hand, so successfully that he remains something of a demigod, remembered not least in the Deming Award, the most prestigious national annual prize for quality. He compiled a 14-point plan that is a complete management philosophy, calling for a culture of improvement and enumerating the ways in which it could be created. One was to 'cease dependence on mass inspection' (the traditional method of quality control) and instead to require statistical evidence that quality was built in. He called for vigorous education and

timeline

1897	1940s
The 80:20 principle	Lean manufacturing

Kaizen – small is beautiful

Kaizen (continuous improvement) constantly introduces small, incremental changes to a business. A core part of total quality management, it has since been adopted by lean manufacturing (see page 28). It can be a very effective tool, but it is not one that can be used on its own. It will only work in an organization where everyone from the boss down is encouraged to participate, creating a benign environment for the quality circles (see page 187) that form part of its implementation.

Improvement on a grand scale may seem more attractive - the quantum leap. But quantum leaps are risky and difficult to pull o f, because they affect so many people and processes. Small improvements are easier

(because the ideas come from the people themselves), quicker, cheaper and less risky, and they accumulate to the point where the effect may be greater than the quantum leap. Because this approach encourages workers to take 'ownership' of their work, it can be highly motivating. Management must still be on the lookout for circumstances where dramatic change really is necessary, however, because such change is unlikely to arise from Kaizen.

The popular but misnamed 'Kaizen blitz' – the Japanese call it *kaikaku*, which means 'radical' improvement – is a one-off, localized, smaller-scale improvement when a team drops everything for a week or ten days to improve a process.

training, the breaking down of barriers between departments and the daily involvement of top management. He also advocated continuous improvement by repeating the PDCA cycle – plan (get the data, analyse the problem, plan the solution), do, check (measure the change) and action (modify as necessary).

Joseph M. Duran (see page 68) was another strong American influence. 'Quality does not happen by accident', he said. This was the starting point for his 'quality trilogy' of quality planning, quality control and quality improvement. Kaoru Ishikawa, who gave his name to the 'Ishikawa

1951	1981	1986
Total quality management	Japanese management	Six Sigma

❝We are being ruined by best efforts.❞

Deming's Second Theorem

diagram' or 'fishbone' diagram – a quality problem-solving tool – was another important figure in the development of TQM. Armand Feigenbaum first used the term 'total quality control' in a 1951 book, and the 'control' was later corrected to 'management' by Ishikawa.

Though many elements have been hijacked by later methodologies (see pages 112 and 156), TQM as such has fallen from grace. In its heyday it was an entire way of life for the company and had to be led by top management. When it wasn't – which happened often enough among western companies who would pick the bits they liked – it was almost sure to fail, something that contributed to its shrinking popularity. Though it focused on the individual department, it was designed to apply across the company, not merely in production. It viewed quality and the business process from the customer's point of view, though the 'customer' could be someone in the same company, the person you passed your work on to or whose request you fulfilled.

The Kaizen way TQM had two overriding goals – total customer satisfaction (internal and external), and what later came to be called 'zero defects'. That didn't mean mistakes wouldn't happen, just that the process wouldn't assume a failure rate. The principle of Kaizen (see box) – the Japanese equivalent of 'continuous improvement' – was deeply embedded in TQM and seen as the only way to maintain a high rate of customer satisfaction. Among other core principles were that prevention is better than cure, and it is cheaper to design faults out of products; quality involves everyone; and employees have a key role in spotting quality problems and suggesting improvements.

This last principle produced 'quality circles', another common feature of TQM and a way of empowering the workforce. Since they go hand in hand with Kaizen, they are sometimes called 'Kaizen teams'. These are groups of people, not too large, who do the same sort of work and meet regularly to solve work-related issues - often using Ishikawa diagrams. Guidelines for quality circles include the following:
• They should be voluntary. No one should be press-ganged into joining them.
• They should meet regularly, under the leadership of their supervisor, for about an hour once a week to begin with. The problems they deal with will dictate subsequent frequency.

• They should meet in normal working hours, but away from distractions of the workplace.
• Each meeting should have a clear agenda and goal.
• The circle must be able to call in expert help if it needs it, and should have its own budget.

As TQM flooded into the US, Phil Crosby, a former quality control manager on the Pershing missile project, packaged many of these ideas for an American audience. He coined the term 'zero defects' and one of his catchphrases was 'do it right the first time'. He also formulated the four absolutes of quality management:

> **Quality has to be caused, not controlled.**
> **Phil Crosby, 1986**

1. Quality is conformance to requirements.
2. Quality prevention is preferable to quality inspection.
3. Zero defects is the quality performance standard.
4. Quality is measured in monetary terms – the price of non-conformance.

He too thought management had to take prime responsibility for quality and introduced quality circles in the form of 'quality improvement teams', encouraging employees to set their own quality goals. He reckoned that manufacturers spent 20% of their revenues doing things wrong and then doing them again, and that service companies could spend up to 35% of operating expenses in the same way. This was the cost of quality. By spending the money on getting it right, they could recoup those costs even before any additional competitive benefits. So 'quality is free' Crosby used to say, using the title of his 1979 book.

TQM was good at optimizing existing processes, but less so when dealing with something new. The methodology assumed that better quality was the answer to all problems, yet many elements survive in other systems and some have detected a large part of it coming back into existence in the new ISO9001 international manufacturing quality standard.

the condensed idea
Zero defects,
100% customer satisfaction

47 Value chain

Michael Porter, who has given management more big ideas than anyone since Peter Drucker, is unyielding on the subject of being competitive. If a company wants competitive advantage, he insists, it must examine every little thing it does through the prism of competitiveness. His five forces model was a tool for assessing the strength of competition outside the factory gate. To help analyse a firm's internal competitiveness, he developed his concept of the value chain.

Porter saw all the interrelated activities that create a product or a service as links in a rather complex chain. Each has a cost, and each adds value to the end product. The firm wants to sell the end product to the customer at a price – an aggregated level of value – that exceeds the sum of the costs. The difference will be its profit margin. To maximize that difference, Porter urged companies to analyse the competitiveness of each link in the chain. He divided the firm's activities into two types:

Primary activities are directly concerned with making the product or delivering the service. These comprise:
- inbound logistics – receiving and storing raw materials from suppliers, and then distributing them to where they are needed;

> **'Value is what customers are willing to pay.'**
> **Abraham Maslow, 1943**

- operations – assembling or manufacturing the finished product, or delivering the service;
- outbound logistics – storing and distributing the finished products;
- marketing and sales – activities aimed at persuading the customer to buy the product, including pricing, channel selection and advertising;
- service – support for customers after they have bought the product, including installation, after-sales service and complaints handling.

timeline

1950

Supply chain management

MICHAEL PORTER (b.1947)

A colleague at Harvard Business School has described Michael Porter as 'probably the world's most influential business academic', and there are many who would regard the 'probably' as redundant. No other management thinker, alive or dead, comes as close to Peter Drucker in terms of the respect he commands.

Porter and Drucker are very different creatures. Drucker, the visionary, always put people at the centre of his philosophy. Porter doesn't really do people but is an academic all the way to the end of his fingertips – relentlessly analytical and averse to showmanship. Harvard made him a University Professor – a rare honour – and created the Institute for Strategy and Competitiveness, dedicated to furthering his work.

That work, with competitiveness at its centre, has radiated outwards from the corporation to whole countries. *The Competitive Advantage of Nations* appeared in 1990 and he has since published standalone competitive studies of New Zealand, Switzerland, Sweden and Canada – leveraging some competitive advantage of his own. He has long been acknowledged as one of the world's highest-paid academics.

As part of his work on national competitiveness he has highlighted the value of industrial 'clusters' – like Hollywood, Silicon Valley or Cambridge's Silicon Fen. Other areas that have caught his interest include inner city development, rural development, corporate social responsibility and innovation. Of his 17 books, the most recently published are *Redefining Health Care* and *Can Japan Compete?* (Answer: yes, if it repents of bureaucratic capitalism.) Japan now awards an annual Porter Prize for achievement in strategy.

Support activities help to improve the efficiency or effectiveness of the primary activities. These are:
- procurement – the purchasing of all goods, raw materials and services needed to create the product or service (the 'value-creating' activities);
- technology development – research and development, automation and other use of technology to support value-creating activities;
- human resource management – recruiting and selecting employees, training, developing, motivating and paying them;

• firm infrastructure – organization and control, finance, legal and information tecnology.

The firm can gain competitive advantage by carrying out these strategically important activities more cheaply or better than its competitors. The activities are connected by linkages, through which the performance or cost of one affects another. These linkages are very important, and include flows of information as well as goods and services. Marketing and sales, for example, must deliver timely and realistic sales forecasts to different departments. Only then can procurement order the right quantities of raw materials to arrive on the right date. Inbound logistics will be prepared and operations can schedule production so that deliveries can be met.

Another example of linkages in action would be if a product were redesigned to reduce manufacturing costs – but then was found inadvertently to have increased service costs. The more efficiently the firm can perform value chain activities and manage its linkages, the more it will boost its margin – or, as Porter would say, 'generate superior value'.

Understanding costs Value chain analysis is useful in pursuing either of Porter's two generic competitive strategies – cost advantage or differentiation. Its focus on separate activities should lead to a better understanding of cost, and how to squeeze it out of a particular part of the chain. It also helps the company to decide which activities it can perform better than its competitors, suggesting opportunities for differentiation. Value chain analysis can also highlight activities where outsourcing might be a sensible option.

The firm can build a cost advantage by reducing the cost of individual activities in the value chain, or by reconfiguring the value chain. Reconfiguring might mean introducing a new production process or new distribution channels. For instance, Federal Express reconfigured its value chain, and transformed the express freight business, by buying its own planes and developing a hub and spoke structure.

Porter picked out a number of factors that could affect cost in value chain activities. They include: economies of scale, capacity utilization, linkages among activities, learning, interrelationships among business units, degree

> **Performing similar activities better than rivals may be essential to superior performance, but tends to drive companies to competitive convergence rather than uniqueness.**
> **Michael Porter, 1985**

of vertical integration, timing of market entry and geographic location. Control these more effectively than your competitors and you can create a cost advantage.

A firm that has chosen to differentiate can look for advantage in any part of the value chain. In procurement, for example, a rare or unique input could create differentiation. So could distribution channels that offer high levels of customer service. Reconfiguring the value chain to achieve differentiation might involve some form of vertical integration – acquiring a customer or supplier. Uniqueness is what differentiation is all about – but differentiation demands creativity and can often cost more.

Porter singled out various drivers of uniqueness, noting that many of them were also cost drivers. They included: policies and decisions, linkages, timing, location, interrelationships, learning, integration and scale. A firm's value chain is not an island. It is part of a wider system of value chains – those of suppliers, of channels and customers. Together they make up what Porter calls the 'value system'.

Linkages exist between the chains, and they may be more or less formalized. Vertical integration – acquiring suppliers or customers – can help to extend control here, but coordination is possible in other ways. Motor component suppliers might agree to build their plants close to a car manufacturer, for example. In much the same way as it must manage internal linkages, a firm's ability to create and keep a competitive advantage will also depend on how well it is able to manage external linkages, and to manage the whole value system of which it is a part.

the condensed idea
Links to competitiveness

48 War and strategy

The idea that business could be warfare by another name took hold of many business leaders during the 1980s. It was not that they wanted to destroy the enemy – though some of them undoubtedly did – but that they believed they should strategize like successful generals.

Though it's no longer fashionable to admit it, many leaders of big businesses have felt an affinity with famous generals. They recognize them as the doers of their time, in an age when 'trade' was not a respectable calling. Born later, the kind of men who rose to generalship might well have opted for industry instead. They would have found themselves doing much the same job, planning, organizing resources and motivating large groups of people to reach a defined objective.

> **❝In strategy everything is very simple, but not on that account very easy.❞**
>
> **Carl von Clausewitz, 1832**

Jack Welch, General Electric's reforming ex-CEO, made no secret of his admiration for Carl von Clausewitz, whose writings were said to have 'distilled Napoleon into theory'. He was the Prussian chief-of-staff at Waterloo, and his *On War* was published posthumously in 1832. 'Strategy forms the plan of the war', Clausewitz wrote, but acknowledged the truth that plans may have to change. So strategy had to go 'with the army to the field in order to arrange particulars on the spot', he added. 'Strategy can never take its hand from the work for a moment.'

As the quote suggests, Clausewitz's approach to strategy was descriptive rather than prescriptive, which appeals to Welch. Welch once quoted from a letter written by one of his managers, saying it captured much of his own thinking about strategic planning:

timeline

500BC	AD1897
War and strategy	Mergers and acquisitions

'*Clausewitz summed up what it had all been about . . . Men could not reduce strategy to a formula. Detailed planning necessarily failed, due to the inevitable frictions encountered: chance events, imperfections in execution, and the independent will of the opposition. Instead, the human elements were paramount: leadership, morale, and the almost instinctive savvy of the best generals. Strategy was not a lengthy action plan. It was the evolution of a central idea through continually changing circumstances.*'

Boston Consulting Group was sufficiently intrigued by Clausewitz to have published a book on him. It was not a Prussian soldier, however, but a Chinese general that best captured the imaginations of late 20th century Western bosses. Beleaguered as they were under the onslaught (more military language) of Japanese imports, they looked East for clues on how to fight back. Japanese literature didn't have much on record, but China offered the extraordinary *Art of War* by Sun Tzu. He was a highly successful general during the later Chou dynasty, and his book – if he wrote it, which is unclear – dates from around 500 BC, when philosophers Confucius and Lao Tzu were both alive.

Aphorism heaven Long admired by Western soldiers, the work is an examination of strategy, teeming with aphorism and insight for even the casual reader. In 13 chapters, Sun Tzu takes us through strategic planning and development, manoeuvring,

> **'It is more fitting to say Art of War than Science of War.'**
> **Carl von Clausewitz,** 1832

spontaneity in the field, dealing with confrontation itself and, finally, the use of intelligence. Strategy is the 'Great Work' of the organization, he insists, and its study cannot be neglected. It has five working fundamentals:
• Tao – the feeling of shared ideals among the group that makes them not fear danger.
• Nature – day, night, hot, cold and the passage of time.
• Situation – near, far, obstructed or easy and the chances of life or death.
• Leadership – intelligence, credibility, humanity, courage and discipline.
• Art – flexibility.

1938
Leadership

1965
Corporate strategy

Sun Tzu said it

He will win who knows when to fight and when not to fight. He will win who knows how to handle both superior and inferior forces. He will win whose army is animated by the same spirit throughout all its ranks. He will win who, prepared himself, waits to take the enemy unprepared. He will win who has military capacity and is not interfered with by the sovereign.

The art of using troops is this:
When ten to the enemy's one, surround him;
When five times his strength, attack him;
If double his strength, divide him;
If equally matched you may engage him;
If weaker numerically, be capable of withdrawing;
And if in all respects unequal, be capable of eluding him, for a small force is but booty for one more powerful.

To fight and conquer in all your battles is not supreme excellence. Supreme excellence consists in breaking the enemy's resistance without fighting.

Sun Tzu acknowledges that war is not independent of politics and economics. Indeed, the five most decisive elements for war are politics, timeliness, favourable geographical location, commanders and law – and politics is the most important. Striking a contemporary chord is his belief that battles should be won with the least cost. The best way to win is through political strategy. He is also insistent that knowledge of the enemy's strengths is at least important as knowledge of your own – use spies.

Lessons for managers? The appearance of the *Art of War* as a CEO primer has triggered many commentaries and 'Management lessons from . . .' books – at least 50, by one reckoning. One is Mark McNeilly's *Sun Tzu and the Art of Business*, in which McNeilly extracts from the work six strategic principles for managers.

1. Capture your market without destroying it. Head-on confrontation should be avoided if at all possible. Price wars draw the quickest and most aggressive responses from competitors, and leave everyone drained of profits.

'*Generally in war, the best policy is to take a state intact; to ruin it is inferior to this . . . For to win 100 victories in 100 battles is not the acme of skill. To subdue the enemy without fighting is the acme of skill.*'

2. Avoid your competitor's strength and attack their weakness.
'*An army may be likened to water, for just as flowing water avoids the heights and hastens to the lowlands, so an army avoids strength and strikes weakness.*'

3. Use foreknowledge and deception to maximize the power of business intelligence.
'*Know the enemy and know yourself. In a hundred battles you will never be in peril.*'

4. Use speed and preparation to overcome the competition swiftly. Speed is not haste – it requires much preparation
'*To rely on rustics and not prepare is the greatest of crimes. To be prepared beforehand for any contingency is the greatest of virtues.*'

5. Use alliances and strategic control points to 'shape' your competitors and make them conform to your will.
'*Those skilled in war bring the enemy to the field of battle and are not brought there by him.*'

6. Develop your character as a leader to maximize the potential of your employees.
'*When one treats people with benevolence, justice and righteousness, and reposes confidence in them, the army will be united in mind and all will be happy to serve their leaders.*'

While Sun Tzu continues to have a following, generals are being put out to grass as strategic role models and their places taken by, among others, sports teams.

the condensed idea
Strategy lessons from the military

49 Web 2.0

With a few far-sighted exceptions, business is slow to wake up to the new. When it does, however, it devours it. A handful of early movers turn a new idea into a competitive advantage until everyone else catches up. Then the new becomes the norm and the field is levelled once again. That is as true for communications technology as for anything else, perhaps more so – business turned the telegraph, telephone, telex and fax machine to its purposes. Now comes the Internet and all that flows from it. But some believe (the most dangerous four words in the business vocabulary, others say) that 'this time it's different'.

Ideas about the communications possibilities of packet-switching and networking surfaced at MIT in the early 1960s, and the first network with computers communicating over a phone line was built in 1965. But it was the 1980s before business began to scent possibilities, and the first Interop trade fair showcasing the Internet was in 1988. The Internet is the underlying, enabling network, but business was more interested in the applications you could park on top of it, notably the email messaging system and the Web, which shares information by using browsers to access Web pages.

Companies quickly cottoned on to the virtues of email as a medium for communications, though its use as a marketing channel has been impaired by floods of spam. They, and their customers, were more tentative about the Web and many inaugural corporate websites were information-only. It was in the more sheltered environment of business-to-business transactions that e-commerce first began to gain traction. As consumer anxieties over

timeline

early 1950s	1958	1964
Channel management	Tipping point	The four Ps of marketing

security faded, and as satisfactory online purchases of books or holidays bolstered confidence, e-tail finally came into its own, spreading to every conceivable corner of the retail trade. With lower transaction costs translated into lower prices, online shopping grew by 50% in 2006 to account for 10% of all UK retail sales, though in the US its share is still around 3%. For agile manufacturers and some service providers this may simply have meant focusing on a new distribution channel (see page 32). But the media have felt the icy blast as more people choose to stay informed via blogs and social networking sites such as MySpace, instead of print and TV.

One click and they're off Web clearly isn't going to destroy bricks-and-mortar but, even in the US, many who still shop offline are effectively making their purchasing decisions online, clicking their way from site to site, comparing prices and specs. The reverse of that coin is that some shops are becoming more like showrooms, as customers come in to feel the goods, and then purchase online. 'Googling' a company or a product has become part of the language and, for many, an integral part of shopping and finding information. Companies need not only a Web presence but one that's 'sticky' (see page 180), or one click and they're off. The Web is the most selfish environment in the world, as they like to say at Yahoo!

[The internet] is enabling a new business architecture that challenges the industrial-age corporate structure as the basis for competitive strategy.

Don Tapscott, 2001

The bursting of the dot.com bubble knocked the breath out of the new economy – for a short while – and seemed to vindicate those who felt the online revolution had been overhyped. Among them was the estimable Michael Porter. He dismissed the view that the Internet was a break from the past, insisting it was merely part of the ongoing evolution of IT, on a par with scanning and wireless communications. Don Tapscott, coauthor of *Digital Capital*, disagreed completely, arguing that Internet was already changing dramatically. He called it the new infrastructure of the 21st century – 'the mechanism by which individuals and organizations exchange money, conduct transactions, communicate facts, express insight and opinion, and collaborate to develop new knowledge'. While Porter

1980	**1983**	**2004**
The five forces of competition	Globalization	Web 2.0
		The long tail

catchy virus

Viral marketing, that elusive spread of a message through the population like a contagion, is getting harder. Advertisers jostle for attention on websites and the Web community grows ever more cynical. For any old economy marketing manager still brave enough to try, Karl Long, blogger (and Web integration manager for Nokia's video game group), points out that success bears no relation to investment. He suggests a three-step approach:

Experiment – treat it as an innovation exercise, building a portfolio of social media experiments through blogs, vlogs, podcasts, widgets, social networks (tools that are easy to engage with and share). Failure is not only an option, it's a requirement. 'Fail faster so you can succeed sooner.'

Monitor – social media put a plethora of tools in marketers' hands allowing real-time measurement and monitoring of your ideas in the marketplace. Technorati, del.icio.us, BlogPulse, PubSub are just a few tools to see what ideas are being shared, and what ideas are taking off. Monitoring is not just about measurement, though – it's about listening. Pay attention to the conversations, responses and mashups and you'll have a rich source to draw from when you . . .

Respond – when things take off, you had better be ready to respond, participate and engage in the ensuing conversation. Can you amplify what's happening, can you reflect what's happening, can you capitalize on what's happening? Have fun, have a sense of humour. There is really only one rule of viral marketing, and that's 'don't take yourself too seriously'.

believed that universal adoption would 'neutralize' the Internet as a source of competitive advantage, Tapscott countered that it would allow companies to create unique products, wring out waste, differentiate themselves and reach new suppliers and customers. In fact, the Web is already a very different creature from its original, relatively passive page-oriented self. They were places to visit. Today the Web is a place you go to get things done. Enter Web 2.0.

Participation, not publishing Tapscott was right in his assertion that the Web was becoming more than a cross between a shopping arcade and the *Yellow Pages*. If Web 1.0 was publishing, Web 2.0 is participation, says publisher Tony O'Reilly (whose company helped articulate this phase two concept in 2004). A 'wiki' website is very Web 2.0, allowing users to add to or edit its content (*wiki-wiki* is Hawaiian for 'quick'). The best-known example is Wikipedia, the online encyclopedia that anyone can amend, sometimes to its detriment, but some firms are using wikis to create pre-meeting agendas or to develop ideas. In some, wiki traffic now exceeds intranet traffic.

Mashups Web 2.0 sites have the software and the data to do things for you, instead of having to download software packages to do it yourself. The Web looks ever more web-like and linkage is key too, either by connecting people through social networking sites and blogs, or by combining different sources of content on the same site – 'mashups'. A mashup was used to help New Orleans residents, displaced by Hurricane Katrina, to find jobs – they typed the kind of job they were looking for into the site, which searched over 1,000 job boards and displayed their location on a Google map. 'Viral marketing' (see box) tries to exploit social linkages to create 'word of mouth' awareness of products or services across the Web.

Web 2.0 companies such as eBay and Skype, were born on the Web. Whenever someone uses them and leaves a comment or adds a contact, they are improving the tool for themselves and for everyone else. 'Every time we go on these sites we're programming the web,' Tapscott notes. However, non-Web companies are still feeling their way around Web 2.0. A few have established a presence inside Second Life, one of the Web's digital worlds. Penguin, the publisher, has, perhaps rashly, launched a wiki novel project, called *A Million Penguins*, which has attracted varying levels of talent. Innovation opportunities clearly exist, though the Web community needs careful handling. But research suggests brands that succeed on the Web generate emotional ties, becoming 'owned' not only by the people who create them but also by the people who use them.

> **'eBay's product is the collective activity of all its users; like the web itself, eBay grows organically in response to user activity.'**
>
> **Don Tapscott,** 2001

the condensed idea
The new infrastructure of the 21st century

50 What business are you really in?

Every once in a corporate blue moon a truly revolutionary idea comes along, one that makes every thinking company look at what it is doing through a new pair of spectacles. And a vision corrective was exactly what Theodore Levitt offered managers with his scornful, provocative and hugely influential article 'Marketing myopia', when it appeared in the *Harvard Business Review* in 1960. Its subject may have been marketing but, as much as anything, it was about strategy.

There is surely not a business in the developed world that doesn't 'focus on the customer', or at least claim to. So it may be hard to remember, or conceive of, a time when that simply wasn't so. But that's just how it was at the start of the 1960s, when Levitt chose to shake US industry by the scruff of its collective neck. He began by pointing out that every major industry was once a growth industry. Some still were, but had the spectre of decline looming over them. Others had already stopped growing. In either case, the reason was not market saturation but a failure of management, right at the top. His Exhibit A is worth quoting in full:

> **The best way for a firm to be lucky is to make its own luck.**
> **Theodore Levitt, 1960**

'The railroads did not stop growing because the need for passenger and freight transportation declined. That grew. The railroads are in trouble today not because that need was filled by others (cars, trucks, airplanes, and even telephones) but because it was not filled by the railroads themselves. They let

timeline

1450
Innovation

1938
Leadership

THEODORE LEVITT 1925–2006

Economist and Harvard professor Theodore Levitt assured his place in contemporary management history with 'Marketing myopia'. The article, one of 25 he wrote over time for the *Harvard Business Review,* combined his talents as an adventurous thinker and a zesty writer. Readers thought so too – more than 1,000 companies ordered 35,000 reprints in the weeks after publication and the total has since risen to 850,000.

Born in Germany, he moved to Dayton, Ohio with his family aged ten. He co-founded a newspaper while still at elementary school, and later worked as a sports reporter on the local paper, finishing high school by correspondence – his education had been interrupted by the Second World War and the army. He caught up rapidly, gaining a PhD in economics and, after working as an oil consultant, he moved to Harvard in 1959 where he remained for the rest of his professional life.

Levitt not only wrote for the *Harvard Business Review* but edited it from 1985 to 1990, making it less academic and a lot more popular. If he hadn't written 'Myopia', he might still be remembered for having popularized the word 'globalization'. He used it in a 1983 paper entitled 'The globalization of markets'.

others take customers away from them because they assumed themselves to be in the railroad business rather than in the transportation business. The reason they defined their industry incorrectly was that they were railroad-oriented instead of transportation-oriented; they were product-oriented instead of customer-oriented.'

Entertainment, not movies Hollywood had survived the birth of television, but only by the skin of its teeth. All the big studios had gone through drastic reorganizations and some had disappeared. The cause of their troubles, however, was not television's inroads but the studios' myopia. They thought they were in the movie business when they were really in the entertainment business. They dismissed television when they

1960
What business are you really in?

1965
Corporate strategy

1990s
Customer relationship management

should have welcomed it as an opportunity. Levitt asked: 'Had Hollywood been customer-oriented (providing entertainment) instead of product-oriented (making movies), would it have gone through the fiscal purgatory it did?' He doubted it.

> **The difference between marketing and selling is more than semantic. Selling focuses on the needs of the seller, marketing on the needs of the buyer.**
>
> **Theodore Levitt, 2001**

Levitt insisted that there is no such thing as a growth industry, only companies that can create and capitalize on growth opportunities. Dead and dying 'growth' industries had believed in one or more of these four myths:
- our growth is assured by an expanding and more affluent population;
- there is no competitive substitute for our industry's major product;
- we can protect ourselves through mass production and rapidly declining unit costs as output rises;
- excellence in technical research and development will ensure our growth.

Levitt noted that a growing market keeps the manufacturer from having to think very hard or imaginatively. If your product has an automatically expanding market, you may be tempted not to think about how to expand it yourself. He berated the oil industry for believing in the first two myths and for concentrating on improving the efficiency of getting and making its product, rather than improving the generic product or its marketing.

Bye-bye buggy whip There is no guarantee against product obsolescence, he warned, and if a company's own research doesn't make a product obsolete, someone eise's will. With the advent of the automobile, no amount of product development was going to save the buggy whip industry. Had it thought of itself as being in the transportation industry, however, it might have turned to making, say, fan belts.

In mass production industries, Levitt noted that volume can be a snare and a delusion. 'The prospect of steeply declining unit costs as output rises is more than most companies can usually resist . . . All effort focuses on production. The result is that marketing gets neglected.' A fixation with research and development can be as dangerous, producing the illusion that superior product will almost sell itself. Again, marketing is a neglected afterthought, the uncared for stepchild. In all these instances, companies think of themselves as producing goods and services, not customer satisfactions. They should be thinking the reverse. 'An industry begins with the customer and his or her needs, not with a patent, a raw material or a selling skill.' Having started with the customer's needs, an industry should develop backwards, through delivery, creation and, finally, finding the raw materials.

Selling is not marketing Levitt didn't mean that selling was being ignored. 'But selling, again, is not marketing', he said. 'Selling concerns itself with the tricks and techniques of getting people to exchange their cash for your product. It is not concerned with the values that the exchange is all about. And it does not, as marketing invariably does, view the entire business process as consisting of a tightly integrated effort to discover, create, arouse and satisfy customer needs.'

> **'People actually do not buy gasoline. What they buy is the right to keep driving their cars.'**
> **Theodore Levitt, 1960**

Levitt said that building an effective, customer-oriented company involved far more than good intentions or promotional tricks. It involved profound matters of human organization and leadership. The company needed a 'vigorous', driven leader, one with a vision than could produce eager followers in vast numbers. 'In business, the followers are the customers.'

In Levitt's refocused company, management has to think of itself not as producing products but as providing customer-creating satisfactions, and it has to push that idea – and everything it means – into every corner of the organization. It must think of itself as 'buying customers' and it's the chief executive who has responsibility for creating this attitude and aspiration. 'The chief executive must set the company's style, its direction and its goals', Levitt concluded. 'This means knowing precisely where he or she wants to go and making sure the whole organization is enthusiastically aware of where that is. This is a first requisite of leadership, for unless a leader knows where he is going, any road will take him there.'

the condensed idea
The company is a customer-satisfying organism

Glossary

Amortized cost The value of assets wastes away, so their cost is charged against profits – amortized – over a number of years. The more years, the smaller the annual charge.

Barriers to entry/exit Factors that prevent new competitors from entering a market, or existing ones from leaving it. Usually related to cost or know-how – hence 'cost of entry'.

Bricks and clicks Joint use of the web and physical outlets as complementary distribution channels. Sometimes called 'clicks and mortar'.

Capital Financial or physical assets used to produce an income. Includes money invested in a business (share capital) or borrowed by it (loan capital). Investors expect a return on [the] capital [they have] invested (ROCI).

Clicks and mortar *see* Bricks and clicks

Commoditized Describes products where no single brand has any differentiating features and consumers buy on price alone.

Conglomerate A collection of companies in unrelated businesses, usually owned by a 'holding company'. No longer favoured by investors.

Consolidation In an industry, a reduction in the number of competitors as the bigger ones acquire or eliminate the smaller ones.

Convergence Buzzword of the 1990s, describing the growing interdependence of telecommunications, computers and the media. 'Strategic' convergence is the growing similarity of individual corporate strategies.

Core business The business at the heart of an organization's success. Likewise, 'core' products and 'core' skills. These should never be outsourced.

Cost of entry *see* Barriers to entry/exit

Disclosure Providing relevant information on trading activities, financial performance, assets and liabilities to shareholders and other interested parties.

Efficiency vs effectiveness Efficiency is saving time, money or effort ('doing things right' – Peter Drucker). Effectiveness is doing a quality job that achieves its goals ('doing the right things').

Entrepreneur Someone who undertakes (from the French *entreprendre* – to undertake) to supply the market for a profit. Implies a spirit of initiative and risk-taking.

Ethical investment An investment style that avoids shares in 'unethical' companies, such as those in arms or tobacco, or heavy polluters. For some, corporate governance is also an 'ethical' issue.

5S Japanese system of order and cleanliness in the workplace – *seiri* (tidiness), *seiton* (orderliness), *seiso* (cleanliness), *seiketsu* (standards) and *shitsuke* (sustaining discipline).

Flattening *see* Hierarchical organization

Flotation *see* IPO

Function A distinct department of the business, usually with its own budget, such as sales, production, marketing, human resources and finance.

Goodhart's Law In essence, when a measure becomes a target it stops being a good measure, because it changes the focus of people's activity.

Hierarchical organization An organization with many layers of management, often pyramid-like, with each reporting upwards until they reach the top. 'Flattening' is removing some of these layers.

Inventory Stocks of supplies, work in progress or finished products within the company at any one time.

IPO Initial public offering. Inviting the public to invest in a company's shares for the first time. Otherwise known as 'flotation', 'listing' or even 'getting quoted'.

Listing *see* IPO

Logistics Technically, managing the flow of materials and information along the supply chain, but often used, more specifically, to mean transport and storage.

Margin Profit as a percentage of sales. High margin is good, low margin less so.

Mass customization Adapting a mass-produced product for individual consumption.

Metrics Jargon for 'measurements'.

Multinationals Companies with operations established in more than one country. Some now prefer to think of themselves as 'global companies'.

NGO Non-governmental organization, usually with altruistic purpose. Often involved in stakeholder and corporate social responsibility issues.

Niche A smaller portion of a larger market. Niche marketing is much more targeted than mass marketing.

Non-correlated Describes businesses or investments whose cycles are not related to each other. Since their fortunes are less likely to rise and fall simultaneously, non-correlation should smooth out volatility.

Non-executive director A board director who is not employed as an executive by the company. An 'independent' non-exec is expected to represent shareholders' interests. A non-exec who used to work for the company is not 'independent'.

'Not invented here' syndrome Resistance to any idea or practice that comes from outside the company, or even outside the department.

Offshoring Moving a company operation, often manufacturing, to another country. Not the same as outsourcing, which is to subcontract an operation to someone else, onshore or offshore.

Penetration Market penetration is entering a new market. Penetration pricing is low initial pricing to win consumer acceptance.

Productivity The amount of output per unit of input – often the number of hours required to produce a product. Raising productivity is one of management's favourite preoccupations.

Resources People, equipment, facilities, money and materials used to achieve a particular goal. The trouble with resources is that they are finite.

SBU Strategic business unit. A subsidiary, division or even product within the company that serves its own market and determines its own strategy.

Shareholder value More money for shareholders. This may be in the form of a higher share price, larger dividends or one-off cash payments.

Skimming A pricing strategy for new products, particularly if they are unique. Skimming charges as much as the market will bear, then lowers prices as competitors appear.

Skunk works A small group of experts who work outside strict company rules and often in secret to develop a new product or technology.

Street furniture Equipment placed on or near streets, such as bus shelters, signs, benches and kiosks, which became a new medium for outdoor advertising.

Sustainable development What the behaviour of large companies is expected to promote, so that present behaviour doesn't impair the ability of future generations to meet their own needs. Principally, but not exclusively, environmental.

Synergy The ability of one plus one to equal three. The added value created (or, more often, hoped for) when two companies or activities are joined together.

Unit costs The cost to produce one of something. Economies of scale say that the more of that something you produce, the lower the unit cost will be.

Venture capital Funding for startup or young, high-growth businesses which may be too risky to attract affordable capital from other sources. High-risk, high-reward stuff.

Vertical integration What happens when a company extends its control further along the supply chain, by acquiring either its suppliers (backward integration) or its customers (forward integration).

Viral marketing A technique that encourages people to pass along a marketing message via social networks (word of mouth and electronic), as a virus might spread from person to person. If the pass-along rate is high, the campaign snowballs; if it is low, the message fizzles out.

Index

Bold pagination indicates glossary entry

A

acquisitions 54, 66, 136–9, 164, 166
activity-based costing 53
adhocracy 4–7
advertising 28, 91, 132, 134–5, 181, 196, 198
agency problem 65
alliances 38, 164–7, 195
Amazon 64, 67, 122
Ansoff, H. Igor 49–50, 64
Athos, Anthony 100, 141, 142
authenticity 110–11

B

balanced scorecard 8–11
benchmarking 12–15, 147
Bennis, Warren G. 4, 75, 109–11
blue ocean strategy 16–19
Borden, Neil H. 89, 135
Boston matrix 20–3, 81
brand 28–31, 66, 67, 87, 133, 134, 199
business process
  balanced scorecard 10
  outsourcing 145–6
  reengineering 24–7, 107, 159

C

cash cows 21
Caux Principles 160–1, 162
Chandler, Alfred 61, 98
channel management 32–5, 58
communication 50–1, 58–9, 74, 104, 117, 118, 149, 196
competition
  80:20 law 71
  five forces 51, 84–7, 96
  knowledge economy 105, 107, 109–10
  strategy 51, 67, 195, 202
  value chain 188–91
complexity 52–5, 175
conglomerates 64–6, 137, **204**
core competence 36–9, 51, 145, 161, 166, 202
corporate governance 40–3
corporate social
  responsibility 44–7
corporate strategy 39, 48–51

costs
  activity-based 53
  agency problem 65
  competition 85, 86, 87
  complexity 52–5
  diversification 66–7
  experience curve 80–3
  project management 150
  reducing 169, 171, 187
  target 19
  value chain 126–7, 190–1
creativity 97–9, 106, 178–9
critical path method 149–50
customer relationship
  management (CRM) 9, 35, 56–9, 146
customer service 74, 135, 141, 142, 188, 191
customers
  brands 30, 31
  choice 33–5, 52, 132–3, 134
  and competition 85–6, 87
  creating 19, 57–8, 166
  long tail theory 121, 122
  loyalty 124–7, 133, 159
  needs 26, 27, 52, 133
  satisfaction 9–10, 59, 115, 133, 156, 186, 202–3

D

decentralization 60–3
deregulation 92
differentiation 85, 86, 96, 133, 191, 198
distribution channels 32–5, 87, 90–1, 122–3, 168, 188, 190, 191, 197
diversification 39, 50, 54, 64–7, 137, 202
DMAIC/DMADV acronyms 157, 159
dogs 22
Drucker, Peter 60, 63, 104, 128–31, 163, 189
Dunbar's number 183
DuPont 61, 132, 149

E

e-commerce 196–9
Edwards Deming, W. 70, 184
efficiency 106, 107, 112, 126, 144, 152, 168, 189, **204**
80:20 principle 68–71
emotional branding 31, 199
emotional intelligence 111
employees
  core competence 39
  CRM 59
  empowerment 72–5, 115, 129, 130, 179, 186
  Japanese management 102, 179, 185

knowledge economy 106–7
loyalty 29, 63, 124, 125–7
market forecasts 78, 79
mergers 137, 138
motivation 74, 108, 110, 131, 176–9, 185, 195
organizational excellence 141–3
outsourcing 144–7
scientific management 72, 152–5
social responsibility 45
value chain 189–90
empowerment 72–5, 115, 129, 130, 179, 186
entrepreneurship 8, 76–9, 98, 109, 142, **204**
ethics 45–7, 73, 79, 131, 161, 162, **204**
excellence 140–3
experience curve 21, 80–3

F

feedback 129, 174–5
financial perspective 9
five forces 51, 84–7
five Ss 115, **204**
Ford 27, 55, 112, 154, 169
four Ps 88–91, 135
Friedman, Milton 44

G

General Electric 22, 39, 96, 108, 130, 132, 135, 192
General Motors 8, 27, 55, 60, 69, 103, 118, 130, 132, 169
globalization 92–5, 105, 171, 201
goals 128–31, 135
Google 64, 67, 134, 197
group behaviour 182–3
growth 10–11, 20, 65, 66–7, 164, 202

H

Hammer, Michael 24, 27, 159
Handy, Charles 6, 130
Henderson, Bruce 20, 81
Herzberg, Frederick 178
Hewlett-Packard 78, 108, 141, 142–3, 144
hierarchical management 54, 61, 63, 143, **204**
Honda 101, 167

I

IBM 70, 76, 141, 142, 144, 167
information technology
  BPR 26–7
  core competence 38
  CRM 56–8

innovation 96, 99
knowledge economy 104, 105, 106, 107, 166
outsourcing 144, 145–6
working from home 63
see also Internet
innovation 96–9
  blue ocean strategy 16–19
  costs 52–5
  disruptive 18
  employee role 74
  knowledge economy 105
  technology 76–7, 198, 199
insourcing 93
Internet
  advertising 134–5
  channel management 32, 33–5, 90, 91
  CRM 58–9
  diversification 64
  globalization 92, 93
  i-mode service 165
  innovation 96
  long tail theory 120–3
  Web 2.0 196–9
intrapreneurship 77
inventory 113, 114, 169–71, 174, 188, **204**

J

Japanese management 12, 69, 70, 100–3, 141, 156, 179, 184–5
see also Kaizen; lean manufacturing
Johnson & Johnson 76, 141, 143
Juran, Joseph M. 69, 70, 185
just-in-time production 113, 114, 115, 169

K

Kaizen 74, 114, 115, 185, 186
Kanban 113, 114, 115
Kanter, Rosabeth Moss 72, 75, 95, 98–9
Kaplan, Robert S. 8, 10, 53
Kim, W. Chan 16, 19, 183
knowledge economy 79, 104–7, 109–10, 117, 118
knowledge management 105–6, 195
knowledge process outsourcing 146
Koch, Richard 51, 54, 70

L

leadership 73, 75, 102, 108–11, 119, 142, 175, 193–5, 203
lean manufacturing 12, 101, 112–15, 158, 185
learning curve 80, 82

learning organization 10–11, 116–19, 126, 172
Levitt, Theodore 92–3, 135, 200–3
licensing 166
lifestyles 133
line management 61
long tail theory 120–3
loyalty 30, 74, 87, 124–7, 133

M
M-form structure 62
mail order 33, 90, 123
management by objectives 128–31
manufacturing
  abroad 94
  costs 53, 66, 80–3
  Japanese 36, 38, 100–2
  knowledge economy 104, 107
  lean 12, 101, 112–15, 158, 185
  scientific management 72, 152–5
  suppliers 85, 86, 99, 114
  value chain 188, 190
market development 50, 78–9, 83, 91, 92, 194–5
market penetration 50, 89, 164, 181, **205**
market segmentation 132–5
market share 21, 22, 83, 85–7, 94, 126, 159, 164
marketing
  audit 135
  blue ocean strategy 16–19
  brands 28–31
  channel management 32–5, 90–1
  costs 53, 66–7
  CRM 58
  four Ps 88–91, 135
  Internet 196–7, 198
  long tail theory 121, 122
  mass 132–3, 134, 202
  strategy 50, 91, 200–3
  tipping point 181–2
  value chain 188, 189
mashups 199
Maslow's hierarchy of needs 176–7
mass market 132, 134, 202
Mauborgne, Renée 16, 19, 183
mergers 54, 65, 66, 136–9, 164, 166
micromarketing 134
Mintzberg, Henry 4–7, 183
mission statement 49, 50, 119
monopsony 85

motivation 74, 108, 110, 129, 131, 176–9, 185, 195
Motorola 156, 157–8, 159, 161
multifunctionalism 61–2
multinationals 66–7, 94–5, 129, **205**

N
needs, hierarchy of 176–7
niche products 120, 134, **205**
98% rule 122

O
objectives, management by 128–31
offshoring 93, 94, **205**
open sourcing 93
organizations
  adhocracy 4–7
  core competence 36–9
  excellence 140–3
  goals 128–9, 131, 135
  learning 116–19, 172
  seven Ss 141
  strategy 200–3
outsourcing 54, 93, 94, 144–7, 169, 171, 190

P
Pareto principle 68–71, 122
partnerships 77, 164, 167, 195
Pascale, Richard 100, 141
Peters, Tom 140, 141, 142, 143
planning 50–1, 192–3
Porter, Michael 15, 16, 48, 51, 84, 86–7, 96, 145, 171, 188–9, 197–8
price
  competition 85–7, 188
  costs link 83
  four Ps 89–90, 135
  targeting 19, 30, 121
privatization 92
problem-solving 174–5, 178–9, 186
Proctor & Gamble 27, 29, 96, 134, 141, 143, 144, 170–1
product
  development 50, 64, 66, 76, 83, 98–9, 159
  lifecycle 30, 98, 135, 202
  marketing 89, 132–3
  quality 156–9, 168, 184–7
productivity 105, 106, 107, 112, 114–15, 126, 142, 154–5, **205**
profits
  80:20 principle 71
  diversification 65, 66

loyalty effect 125–7
social responsibility 44–5, 47, 161–2
value chain impact 188
programme evaluation and review technique (PERT) 149, 150–1
project management 148–51
promotion 91

Q
quality 114, 142, 156–9, 168, 184–7
question marks 23

S
scientific management 72, 152–5
Senge, Peter 116–17, 119, 172–5
seven Ss 141
shamrock organization 6
shareholders
  corporate governance 40–3
  and diversification 65–6
  loyalty 124, 125, 127
  value 51, 166, **205**
Shingo, Shigeo 113–14
single-minute exchange of dies (SMED) 113, 115
Six Sigma 101, 156–9
skimming 89, **205**
Sloan, Alfred P. 60, 62, 132, 161
SMART acronym 131
social responsibility 44–7, 161, 162
stakeholders 160–3, 169
stars 22
stock levels 113, 114, 169–71, 174, 188
strategic alliances 38, 164–7, 195
strategic business units (SBUs) 20–3, 36, 38–9, **205**
strategic management 49–50, 160
strategy
  balanced scorecard 8–11
  blue ocean 16–19
  corporate 39, 48–51, 147
  Japanese management 102–3, 185
  management by objectives 129–30
  and marketing 200–3
  seven Ss 141
  Six Sigma 158–9
  and war 48, 192–5
Sun Tzu 193–4

suppliers 85, 86, 99, 114, 144, 169, 188, 189
supply chain management 93, 168–71, 190, 191
systems thinking 172–5

T
tacit interactions 106, 107
takeovers 136–9, 166
Taylor, Frederick W. 72, 130, 152
teamwork 73, 74, 102, 118–19, 131, 155
technology
  costs 52
  CRM 56–9
  disruptive 18
  globalization 92, 93, 94
  innovation 76–7, 96–9
  knowledge economy 105, 166
  value chain 189
technostructure 6
Theories X, Y and Z 176–9
time and motion 152, 154
tipping point 180–3
total quality management (TQM) 101, 184–7
Toyota 103, 112–13
trademarks 29
training 10–11, 54, 79, 106, 110–11, 115–16, 157–8

V
value chain 86, 145, 171, 188–91
value creation 17, 105, 115, 124, 125–7, 137, 139, 145, 189
values, corporate 49, 141
venture capital 77, 99, 109, **205**
viral marketing 198, **205**

W
war, and strategy 48, 192–5
waste 112, 114–15, 152, 169, 187, 198
Waterman, Robert 7, 140, 141, 142, 143
Web *see* Internet
Welch, Jack 108, 192
wiki concept 199

Acknowledgements

A very large thank you to all who helped me on my way, among them friend and management thinker Tom Lloyd, John Bates of the London Business School, consultant Robert Fonteijn, Booz Allen Hamilton's Richard Rawlinson, chef and consultant Sarah Woodward and, *prima inter pares*, Caroline Wood, my agent. But they are not to blame . . .

Dedication

For MP

Quercus Publishing Plc
21 Bloomsbury Square
London
WC1A 2NS

First published in 2007

A catalogue record of this book is available from the British Library

ISBNs
Cloth case edition   ISBN-10: 1 84724 009 7
                      ISBN-13: 978 1 84724 009 5

Printed case edition ISBN-10: 1 84724 150 6
                      ISBN-13: 978 1 84724 150 4

Printed and bound in Dubai, UAE

10 9 8 7 6 5 4 3 2 1

Edited by Keith Mansfield
Designed by Patrick Nugent
Proofread by Carol Baker
Indexed by Ingrid Lock